Live A Life Worth
REMEMBERING

Seeing Change as a Process
for Achieving Your Goals

John J. King Ed.D.

John King Ed.D.

NAPLES, FLORIDA

Live a Life Worth Remembering:
Seeing Change as a Process for Achieving Your Goals
Copyright ©2021 by John J. King Ed.D.

For information on ordering this book in bulk please email the author at
king0558@verizon.net

ISBN: 978-1-7378399-0-3 (Trade Paperback)
ISBN: 978-1-7378399-5-8 (eBook)

Library of Congress Control Number: 2021917720

First Printing 2021
Printed in the United States of America

Cover design by Becky Bayne
Book design and layout by Becky's Graphic Design®, LLC
Edited by Melissa Stevens, Purple Ninja Editorial

This book is dedicated to my wife, Mary, the love of my life, who has stood by me through thick and thin and all the ups and downs during this great adventure called life.

Table of Contents

INTRODUCTION

I recently came across a quote that resonated with me. It quite simply said, "Live a life worth remembering." My life has not been perfect. I have had my ups and downs. I have been a terrible student, and I have earned bachelors, masters, and doctoral degrees. I have been bankrupt and have made enough money to retire and live in Naples, Florida. I have been married, divorced, and remarried. I have had both good and troubled relationships with my children, and I have grandchildren who I adore. I have lost jobs and have secured even better ones. I have enjoyed a great career that has spanned many different opportunities. I have been overweight and lazy, and I have been in perfect shape and have completed nearly fifty marathons. I have traveled extensively throughout the United States and overseas. Through my work and other efforts, I have been blessed with the opportunity to share what I have learned and positively impact the lives of thousands of people. I am now seventy years old and in the final stages of my life, but I can honestly say that I have lived a life worth remembering.

When I was twenty-five my life was in total disarray. I had moved halfway across the country for a job that I did not enjoy. I was in a strange city; I was single and did not know a soul. I was overweight, smoking like a chimney, and abusing alcohol and drugs. I was so lonely, miserable, and unhappy that I would lay awake at night praying I would die so all my pain would end. I knew my life was out of control, but I had no idea what to do about it.

I would head to bars with the idea of meeting people. All I ever got was more desperate and more drunk. One night, actually very early morning, I was returning from one of my trips to the bar when an observant police officer stopped me and invited me to spend a night in his jail. He also gave me an invitation to visit a judge to discuss my lapse in judgment. That wise judge gave me the choice to pay a fine and spend ninety days in the county workhouse or to seek chemical dependency treatment at a local hospital. I thought the hospital option would be the easier of the two as I was not willing to lose my job. In addition, I could not see myself as a jailbird. Little did I know that this would be the beginning of some of the hardest work I would ever do, and it would change my life in ways I never thought possible.

The hospital program promised that if I vigorously and honestly dedicated myself to some simple principles and thoroughly worked twelve simple steps that I would never have to return to living that painful life. It seems like an easy decision, right? Give this new life a try or go back to my miserable life. I jumped in with both feet, and I have never looked back or regretted the choice I made nor the path I have taken.

My path has not always been easy or painless, and it has required a lot of hard work. I have attended numerous twelve-step programs, sat through lots of therapy sessions, read countless self-help books, and attended seminars and workshops galore. Most important of all, it has been the lessons I learned through my mistakes that have allowed me to realize the successes I have achieved. Overall, my life has been one great adventure, and I can see how each experience was necessary to enable me to move on to the next stage.

I have had an interesting career. Every job has taught me something that would help me become a better employee or a skill that would help me move up the ladder. From my most basic jobs as a paperboy, soda jerk, or baloney slicer in a delicatessen to being a C-level executive responsible for hundreds of people and thousands of students, I learned to be responsible, to show up for work, to put in my best effort, and to be a good team member.

This life of mine—that I call well-lived—would not have been possible if I had not been given a process to use when evaluating the challenges and opportunities life presented. Not only have I used this process myself, but I have added additional material learned in my studies on organizational development to help my consulting clients. I will attempt to describe this process through these pages in a way that is simple both to understand and to implement.

Using the steps that I will outline in this book, I have evolved from an overweight, out of shape, chain-smoker who couldn't walk up a flight of stairs into a sensibly eating, non-smoking, healthy individual who exercises, runs daily, and has completed nearly fifty marathons and ultra-marathons. Not bad for a kid whose pre-recovery running career consisted of running to the bathroom and away from trouble.

I am a huge fan of the University of Alabama Crimson Tide football team. During his tenure, head coach Nick Saban has built a successful program that has produced a run of consecutive winning seasons and many national championships. Coach Saban talks about "The Process," the disciplined approach that focuses the team to achieve excellence in all aspects of performance both on and off the field.

The process I will outline can be used for all aspects of one's personal or professional life. The concepts I will describe are by no means my inspired creation. They represent ideas, theories, concepts, and practices that I have been taught or gifted at various points of my education and experience. Many people operate in this manner naturally. Some of us, however, need some guidance and direction to point us to a mode of operation that will help us become happier, more successful people. I hope you find parts or all of this process useful in your life.

I believe that most, if not all, humans experience some malady or dysfunction in their life. This dysfunction does not need to be something as drastic and devastating as alcohol or drug addiction. The issue could be excessive eating, gambling, sexual activity, spending, or any other activity that results in destructive behavior. Some people grow up in an abusive household or become abusive themselves. Some people have problems with their anger or emotions or have psychological conditions. The maladies and dysfunctions can be too numerous to list. I realized that my alcohol, drug, food, and smoking abuses were the result of my emotional and self-worth dysfunction and that my recovery was dependent on me dealing with that dysfunction if I had any hope of staying away from destructive behavior.

If you were intrigued by the title of this book and are reading it right now, then what you, or someone you care about, are doing may not be working. Hopefully, this book will present you with a method that could be used to address the dysfunctions, maladies, or personal demons that are causing some dissatisfaction or unhappiness in life.

If any of what I present or any process you discover is going to be effective, you will need to exert a little faith and a fair amount of work. One of my favorite sayings is: "Faith will move a mountain, but you better bring a shovel." You will need to believe this process will work for you, place some trust in the people and resources you discover to help you through it, and be ready to roll up your sleeves and put in the effort necessary to redirect your life on a path to happiness, serenity, peace, and self-actualization.

The purpose of this book is not to dictate a path that you must take to lead a life well lived but to tell you what worked for me, let you make of it what you will, and take all that you want. If it makes sense, then hopefully I have given you a means to find your own life worth remembering.

CHAPTER ONE

THE CLIFFSNOTES VERSION

"My grandfather invented CliffsNotes.
It all started back in 1912.
Well to make a long story short…"

STEVEN WRIGHT

When you were in high school and had to complete a book report but did not want to read the entire book, you may have consulted a copy of CliffsNotes to get a quick summary of the book's contents without reading through the nuance and detail of the story. I asked a good friend of mine to read this book and tell me what he thought. He suggested that I include a CliffsNotes section for readers who want to know the whole story before they get into the details. I usually take my friend's advice, so this first chapter is my CliffsNotes version of what I would like to communicate to you. If you find it intriguing, I hope you will continue reading to dive deeper into all the nuance and detail.

There is an old saying that the only constant in life is change. If you doubt that, just try to avoid aging. Young children grow before your eyes. Teenagers become more independent. Young adults strike out in the world and become productive citizens. Couples marry and raise families. Even your favorite sports teams change players, coaches, and strategies every year to adapt to changes in the sport and to be more competitive. Organizations change personnel, products, and operational procedures to grow and ensure profits.

Life is a constant cycle of change. We have two choices. We can fight change and remain static and unproductive, or we can embrace change and grow and prosper. The choice is ours.

In his hierarchy of needs, Abraham Maslow (1954) posits that humans continually work to move from their lowest level of need (food and shelter) to their highest level of need (self-actualization). Self-actualization, or reaching your full potential, should be the goal we all seek to achieve. To achieve this goal, we are constantly changing to adjust to the challenges, opportunities, and situations that life presents us with. It is through challenge that we grow.

Throughout my career working with individuals and organizations, I have found that many people, companies, and organizations become static and unproductive because they cannot or will not adjust to the changing conditions in their environment. Change can be scary and intimidating, especially if you lack a process or the knowledge or experience to attack new and challenging situations. Fear has a habit of immobilizing individuals when they should be moving forward.

In my consulting business and my various leadership positions, I have often found that most people and organizations know where they currently are and where they want to ultimately be; however, they lack the process or knowledge of what they need to do to get there. Many years ago, I was working with a woman who owned a business designing jewelry. She was moderately successful but not content with the status of her business or the time and emotional requirements needed to run it. She was trying to decide whether to make her business bigger or to close it down and follow another career choice. In one of our working sessions, she told me that she wished there was a system or process she could follow to analyze her situation and decide which path to take. Together we made a pact that I would develop a process to help her get to the change she desired. Before she was half-way through with the process, she identified the change she wanted to make and was on her way to successfully achieving it. I have subsequently used this process with countless individuals and organizations to achieve successful change.

In any change process, it is logical to assume that most people and organizations will have a general idea of the change they desire. The more specific you can make your vision of this change, the easier it will be to develop a plan to achieve those goals. Professional athletes often talk about visualizing their performance as a way to enhance it. The clearer you can visualize your objective in the change process, the clearer the steps you should take to achieve it will be.

It is also important for both individuals and organizations to be cognizant of the effort they are willing to put into the process, including education or training and any knowledge, special skills, or experience they possess. It may also include the amount of effort and investment they are willing to exert to make the desired change occur, as well as their overall willingness to complete the process and do the work necessary. The basic steps of the process are outlined below and will be covered in depth in the chapters that follow.

Step I: Assess Your Current Situation

After you identify your need for change, the first step in the process is to assess the current situation. It is here that you must come to grips with your immediate environment and circumstances if you are to successfully affect change. How can you know the proper effort necessary for successful change if you're not aware of your current circumstances? Any good business knows that it is important to take a regular inventory. Quite simply, an inventory lets the business take stock of its assets. It lets them know what they have on hand and what they don't. An inventory gives them important information they need to plan for the operation and growth of their business, ultimately determining the value or worth of the company. As an individual, you can inventory your strengths and weaknesses, the things you like about yourself and the things you don't like. Points of pride and current skills can be inventoried as well as those that need to be developed. In essence, a full and thorough assessment is needed to determine what needs to be changed.

Step 2: Eliminate Barriers

Next, eliminate any barriers to change that may exist. There are many obstacles which get in the way of making meaningful change. Fear is one of the most common, but there are many others which keep us from realizing our dreams. A lack of understanding or knowledge often prevents us from achieving our goals. The answer to our problems might be close at hand, but we often let pride or ego get in the way. These barriers do not need to stand in the way. They can be eliminated by honestly evaluating the situation and what needs to change. If you do not eliminate your barriers, successful change becomes extremely difficult, if not impossible.

Step 3: Develop an Action Plan

Once the situation has been assessed, barriers have been eliminated, and a thorough evaluation of those barriers has been conducted, it is time to develop a plan of action. This action plan is your road map, or directions, for getting where you want to go. Individuals who do not adequately plan for change often get lost during the process. Your action plan should include your mission, your defined core values, and your goals. It should also identify any needed information and the steps necessary to achieve your stated goals.

Step 4: Implement the Plan

After your action plan has been honed and refined, it is time to implement. You will never get anywhere on any journey through change if you never start. Sometimes, however, getting started can be the most difficult step of the entire process. The hardest part of any action is the decision to act. Once the process has begun, it's amazing how easy the action itself is to complete, but individuals often become immobilized in trying to get off the dime and begin. Nowhere is this truer than in trying to make changes in life situations. Procrastinating, making excuses, and asking what if questions can result in reasons for doing everything except what really needs to be done.

Step 5: Evaluate the Results

Once you have worked through the process outlined, you should begin experiencing the results of that work. The challenge is then to evaluate those results. Are they what was expected or desired? Do they meet personal needs? Are the results satisfactory? Are there new personal goals that can be achieved? How easy or difficult was the process? Is there anything that could have been done differently or better? Are you in the right place now? It is critical that during the journey the process be kept interesting and motivational to help navigation and progress through the difficult parts of the process.

Step 6: Address the Next Challenge or Opportunity

Once you've evaluated your results, it's time to contemplate what the next challenge or change to be addressed is, or whether a restart of the process is necessary. If any process is to be successful, especially one that is constantly recycling itself, it is essential that information about the success or failure of the process be transferred back for further consideration and refinement. In the context of the process presented here, feedback is vital information about the consequences or end result of the process that is given back to the system to help make better decisions about how change can be realized more effectively and successfully.

I recently read an article in *The New York Times* about Eliud Kipchoge, considered the most prolific marathon runner to date, who just set a world record of two hours, one minute, and thirty-nine seconds at the Berlin Marathon. In that interview, Kipchoge said he follows a personal formula—*motivation* plus *discipline* equals *consistency*—which I think is perfect for thinking about the process of change. If you have the motivation to change and the discipline to thoroughly work the process, you can consistently realize the change you desire. I personally love this formula and have consistently used this change process through all the challenges and opportunities I have encountered with the motivation and discipline to successfully realize change and positive results. If a change is necessary in your life, or in your organization, this is a proven process that can work for you. All that is needed is the courage, the discipline, and the motivation to utilize the necessary input consistently and to work the process that results in the output or change you desire. Good luck!

- **Identify the challenge(s) you wish to overcome or master:**

_____

_____

_____

_____

_____

- **Identify the objectives you hope to achieve:**

_____

_____

_____

_____

- **Identify and eliminate the obstacles that may stand in your way:**

_____

_____

_____

_____

CHAPTER TWO

THE PROCESS

"Hold the vision, trust the process."

ANONYMOUS

A process is defined as a series of actions or steps taken in order to achieve a particular end. For the purpose of this piece, the process is meant to help you develop a better understanding of yourself, your current circumstances, what you desire out of life, and a plan to help you achieve it—in essence to change your present situation into a more desirable one. This process can bring about a change, whether personally or professionally, that can lead to a happier, more fulfilling, well-lived life.

In thinking about this definition of process in relation to change, you may conclude that it is all up to you to make things happen. If you don't do it, change won't occur. In part that is true, but you are part of a bigger whole—the universe, the country, the city, the community, the immediate environment. It is narcissistic to think that the world revolves around you. It is pretty much the opposite. The world revolves with or without you, and you have the choice of getting into the flow of the universe or sitting on the sidelines and watching it pass you by. Everyone exists within the same universe, and there are events and people interacting all around you that you cannot control or influence. Sometimes these people or events can and do have an impact on your environment. You must work this process in conjunction with your environment, and others in it, and that can be either a help or a hindrance.

How much impact, for example, do you have over the local police force in your community? You probably have none, but their actions in providing safety for your community may greatly impact your life, and you may never even be aware of it. How much control do you have over local politicians once you elect them? Once they get on the floor of the assembly, they can vote any way they please; and you can't do much about it until the next election. You send your children to local schools. How much control do you really have over what they are taught and what happens in the classroom? You can tell your employer or supervisor what you think, but how much control do you have over what they do with that information?

When I was in high school, I had a job working in a delicatessen after school and evenings. I remember worrying one summer evening when two suspicious looking men walked into the store, looked around, and left without purchasing anything. There were other customers in the store, and I was busy, so I did not think about it for too long. By the end of the evening, I had completely forgotten about it. I found out the following day that a store owner across the street had seen the men walk into the store and had called the police. The police later had reason to question the men, found a shotgun and a revolver in their vehicle, and discovered that they had robbed a convenience store earlier in the evening. It didn't take too long to figure out that the men were looking over the delicatessen as a possible second robbery site. Were it not for the customers in the deli, the store owner across the street looking out the window and alerting the police, and the subsequent activities of the police officers, who knows what would have happened.

The point is that the interactions of these people and events had a direct effect upon me even though I was not directly involved or responsible for any of them happening. You exist in your environment, which systematically operates through a series of regular, independent, and interdependent activities. Some of these activities impact you more than others. Your responsibility is to act and hope that the environment is well positioned to help you achieve your objectives. You must always be flexible and ready to adjust your plan if necessary.

You operate within systems all the time and are hardly aware of it. The way you get up and start your day in the morning is a system. You may make your bed, take a shower, brush your teeth, get dressed, and have breakfast before you head off for your first activity of the day. If you do this the same way every day, you have a system.

If you look, you can see examples of systems all around you. The earth has a number of systems. The first is in four parts: winter, spring, summer, and fall. We created a calendar to help us manage our lives within that system. The earth orbits the sun, and the moon orbits the earth creating dawn, morning, noon, afternoon, evening, and midnight. We created clocks to help us manage our lives within that system. Plants germinate and bud in the spring; they sprout and grow in the summer. They produce their flowers, fruits, or crops in the fall. They hibernate in the winter and germinate again in the spring. These systems, or cycles, are repeated over and over again. Even you as a person live within a system. You are born and are dependent on your parents during your childhood for nourishment, safety, love, and all the necessities. As you grow, you learn to function, speak, and discover, eventually developing independence during your teen years. In your adult years, you are self-sufficient; you may start your own family and plan for your retirement. Then in your old age, you enjoy the fruits of your labor, and eventually you die.

If you look at life from this viewpoint, you can see that it is nothing more than a series of systems in which you are a participant, responsible for programming what you put into that system, working your process, and realizing the result of that behavior. If you can grasp this concept and begin to focus on how you can and cannot impact your environment and your process, it becomes possible to better program the results you want to achieve. Where most people run into trouble is that they have no clear process to work, or they are following a process that does not get them where they want to go. The balance of this book is dedicated to describing the process the following diagram outlines.

This process looks relatively easy but requires a lot of thought, discipline, and follow-through to ensure that you reach your desired outcome. The process entails the following steps:

- **Identify the challenge(s) you wish to overcome or master:**

  _____

  _____

  _____

- **Identify the objectives you hope to achieve:**

  _____

  _____

  _____

- **Identify and eliminate the obstacles that may stand in your way:**

  _____

  _____

  _____

- **Identify the resources you have, or will need, to achieve your objective:**

  _____

  _____

- **Develop a plan of action you will follow to achieve your goal:**

  _____

  _____

  _____

- **Review your results and, if necessary, revise and implement a renewed plan, or enjoy the results of your efforts.**

The following chapters describe how each of these steps will get you closer to the change, or situation in life, you want and onto the path to a life well lived.

Before undertaking this process, however, you must develop the desire and the discipline to follow through from start to finish. The process is not always easy or painless, and you must be dedicated to achieving your desired goals. If you have the motivation to achieve a meaningful change, and you have the discipline to work a process, then you will be consistent in your effort and improve the likelihood of reaching your goal.

The late congressman John Lewis is quoted as saying, "If you don't do everything you can to change things, then they will remain the same."

Before embarking on this journey, you must ask yourself if you have the drive and discipline to diligently work the process and to be consistent in your efforts. Are you willing to do everything you can to change? If so, it is time to get started.

CHAPTER THREE

IDENTIFYING THE CHALLENGE

"Don't limit your challenges; challenge your limits. Each day you must strive for constant and never-ending improvement."

TONY ROBERTS

*C*ambridge Dictionary defines a challenge as "something that needs great mental or physical effort in order to be done successfully and therefore tests a person's ability." You encounter many situations in life that test your ability and require great mental or physical effort in order to achieve the outcome you desire. Earning masters and doctoral degrees required great mental effort on my part. Completing nearly fifty marathons and ultra-marathons required great physical effort on my part. However, before I was able to embark on either of those journeys, I needed to identify the reason or motivation that would inspire or compel me to attempt either of those efforts. In the case of the graduate degree, it was the desire to advance my career in higher education. As for running, it was the motivation to lose and eventually keep off excessive weight.

I also needed to identify any barriers that stood in the way of my accepting those challenges, such as money, time, self-doubt, etc., and that could potentially interfere with my success. So, too, it is with all of us, if we want to successfully accept and overcome any challenge we face. We must first identify the challenge, the opportunity, or problem to be overcome; our reason or motivation to accept the challenge; and the obstacles that may stand in the way of our success.

In any challenging situation, you are trying to bring about a change. *Webster's Dictionary* defines the verb change as "to make different; to give a different position, course, or direction; to make a shift from one to another; to exchange for an equivalent sum or comparable item; to undergo transformation, transition, or modification." These are all descriptions of action that reference moving from one place to another. If you are to move from one place to another, however, don't you first need to know where you are?

One of the first principles of bringing about successful change is the requirement that you honestly evaluate and accept things as they currently exist. This sounds a lot easier than it actually is. Humans are complex individuals and don't always accept their lives as they are. You can be consciously or unconsciously deluded, either by convincing yourself that things are OK, or by denying that a condition exists at all. Denial, sooner or later, only results in the situation getting worse, or out of control. The alcoholic, for example, denies his or her drinking until it results in job loss, family problems, or even injury. The drug addict may get in trouble with the law. The compulsive gambler may develop serious financial problems or even bankruptcy. What about the person who feels unfulfilled in their job and begins to lose effectiveness because of a lack of interest? Or the person in a bad marriage who stops communicating with their spouse and tunes out to the point where the other party seeks a divorce? How about a person with a cholesterol count of 280 who denies that their improper diet has any effect on their health until the first heart attack hits? What about the business owner or manager who denies that their customers are dissatisfied with the service their firm has been providing until that customer begins to do business with a competitor? We can all come up with rationalizations to defend our behavior, but sooner or later the consequences of denying that problems exist will catch up with us.

I know, for example, in my own business things were not going the way I wanted for a long time before I did anything about it. I was taking on assignments that I really had no business being involved in, and I could not admit that it was a mistake. I could rationalize and justify this action by saying it was for the good of the company and

I would do a good job. But I knew this was not the kind of work I wanted to do. I was not properly suited for the work, and my skills and strengths lay elsewhere. It finally took a crisis for me to realize that something was wrong.

Crisis is a funny thing. Webster's defines a crisis as "a decisive or critical moment." When I really sit down and think about it, most major periods of growth or excitement in my life have been preceded by some crisis. That crisis usually made me look at where I was and helped me decide whether or not I wanted to continue along that path or change to a new direction. What is funny about crisis is how much humans despise it and will do just about anything to avoid it. But if you look at crisis, you see that it is merely an indication that you must make a change, because the direction in which you are headed is too painful or fraught with danger. This is true whether you are looking at yourself as an individual or as an organization. What you must learn to do is embrace the crisis in your life and change your attitude toward it. You must see crisis as a signal, not a punishment. It is a challenge to be overcome, not an insurmountable barrier keeping you from your final goal.

Crisis, in its purist form, is good for us because it helps us move from one place to another. If you didn't have the crisis, in many cases you would never know you need to change. Think about how the body uses pain to make itself change. When you put your hand on a hot stove, for instance, the pain reaction tells you to get your hand off the burner quickly. Your hand is in crisis and in danger of being badly burned, so your brain says it is time to move. Crisis, in the same way, is telling you that what you are doing is not working and that it is time to try something new. Just think about what your life would be like if you never had any crisis. Would you be where you now find yourself?

If you are to overcome the obstacles in your life preventing you from making changes, then you must first come to grips with the reality of the situations causing you concern or even creating fear. There are many barriers that get in the way of making meaningful change or accepting any challenge. Fear, as I have just mentioned, is one of the major ones. I don't know how many opportunities I have missed because I was too afraid to take a risk. How many fun dates with a cute girl did I miss out on because I was too fearful to ask her out because I may be rejected? How many business opportunities did I miss out on because I was too afraid to make a cold call or introduce myself to someone at a networking session? How many times did I let my children, family, friends, or co-workers walk all over me because I was too afraid to set boundaries or confront their behavior?

There are many other barriers which keep us from accepting challenges and realizing our dreams. Ignorance is one of them. Many times a lack of understanding or knowledge prevents us from achieving our goals. The answers to your problems might be close at hand, but you may not know where to look, or are too proud to ask for help. I don't know how many times I have let my ego get in my way. And, in all honesty, I must say that most of the time I have been my own biggest barrier to accepting challenges and realizing meaningful change—I got in my own way.

You do not need to let these barriers stand in your way. You can eliminate them and begin to make the changes you want in your life or in your organization. You start by being honest about yourself and the things you want to change. You also need to look at the affect it is having on your life. It takes a lot of energy and strength to suppress the truth, especially from yourself. If you can release yourself, you can begin to channel that energy into working on the challenge and making change.

When you begin to honestly look at what is going on in your life, you will find that there are many things over which you have no control. It's difficult for many of us to admit that we are powerless over anything. It goes against everything most of us have ever learned. You are supposed to be able to overcome and master anything if you simply put your mind to it. Thinking like that got me into lots of trouble. How would you handle walking through a brick wall if you were to put your mind to it? Would you use your shoulder, or kick your way through it, or maybe literally use your head and try to butt your way through it? Probably not. You would merely end up with sore body parts and still be on the wrong side of the wall. By admitting that the brick wall is stronger than you are, you realize that you cannot go through the wall, but you can figure a way around it. The same logic applies to the first stage of the change process. By admitting that the problem may be too big for you to bully your way through, you can find a better, more successful way around your problem—or rather out of it—instead of continuing to hurt yourself by trying to will your way through it. Thus, by admitting your weakness, you find your strength.

Looking at your past behaviors and the consequences of those behaviors is a critical step. It is a key part of the process because if you do not remember the consequences of your old ways, you will be tempted to go back to them as that is the most comfortable and natural way for us to act. It is the memory of the pain and suffering that prompted us to change in the first place that will motivate us to maintain the changed behavior.

There are three general areas where change usually occurs in your life. You make changes in yourself and how you feel and relate to yourself. You also make changes in your relationships with others. No man is an island, and throughout your life you develop relationships with other people on various levels that greatly impact your life. And, finally, you participate in some form of life work or activity, which makes up a large portion of your time. Early in life you go to school. Later you choose a profession or craft that provides you with a living. You get involved in hobbies, sports, or community events, which help to form your character. You participate in leisure activities, which bring you pleasure and add to your personality. You may devote a portion of your life to raising children or other home-based activities. These activities are constantly changing as you develop and grow as an individual. It is important to identify what challenges you will accept, as well as where and how you want to make changes in your life, so you can take ownership of those changes and begin to develop an action plan that will facilitate the outcome you desire.

As you think about your current situation, it may be helpful to ask yourself some questions as they pertain to you or your organization:

- What challenge(s) do you wish to overcome or master?

  _____

- As a result of these challenges, what changes will occur in you, your relationships, your organization, or your activities—professionally, socially, or at home?

  _____

- What is your reason for wanting to address these challenges?

  _____

- How does your current situation impact your life, either positively or negatively?

  _____

- What specific events led to your current situation?

  _____

- What specific behaviors have led to your current situation?

  _____

- Have you felt out of control or uncomfortable as a result of the current conditions in your life or organization?

  _____

- What harmful consequences have occurred as a result of your current situation—physical, monetary, emotional, legal, etc.?

  _____

- How has this situation impacted others, and what consequences has it introduced into their lives and/or your organization?

  _____

  _____

CHAPTER FOUR

OBJECTIVES

"Objectives are not commands; they are commitments."

PETER F. DRUCKER

Webster's defines a goal as "the end toward which effort is directed: aim." In sports a goal is the score a team or player receives when they successfully complete an action that is the objective of the game. How many times in your life have you fixed your mind on the accomplishment of some purpose, and then when you have achieved that objective, you're elated at your accomplishment? That purpose or objective was what drove you onward when the odds seemed stacked against you. Goals are important to us as human beings, and they are also important to organizations.

Goals are what motivate us to keep moving in a forward direction. If you didn't have goals, or something to aim toward, you would wander around aimlessly trying to figure out where you were going in life. You certainly would not start off a trip in an automobile if you did not know where you were heading. How would you know which direction to head in first? How would you know when to change direction? How would you know when you arrived at your destination? Instead, you figure out where you want to go, and then you might consult a map to figure out the best way to get there. Today that task is a lot easier if you have a navigation system or smart phone in your car. All you need to do is plug in the address, and the system will tell you step-by-step how to get to your destination. You still need to know what the final destination is if you want the navigation system to work properly.

The motivation behind your goals can be either positive or negative. When I first started jogging, my strategy was to make it around the lake near where I was living. Naturally, I was not able to make it around the three-mile circumference of the lake my first time out, so I developed my park bench strategy. I would literally run from one park bench to the next, huff and puff till I caught my breath, and then run from the next park bench to yet another. I kept doing this every day until I could run two park benches and then three and then four. My goal was to put together as many park benches as I could. After weeks of work, I was successfully running about one-third of the lake. One day I was feeling pretty good, and I pushed myself past my normal ending point and attempted to get around the entire lake. I barely made it, but I did make it. From that point on, my goal was to get around the lake without dying from exhaustion. To make it through the last third of my run, I would fantasize that I was finishing a marathon, and I would imagine all of these people lined up along the route cheering me on. It was then that I set a goal of successfully running a marathon someday.

One day I had the opportunity to talk to a fitness trainer at a local health club. I told him of my goal and asked if he had any advice. I was shocked when he told me not to do it, that I might hurt myself, and that it would probably be too hard for me. From that embarrassing moment on, my goal was to prove that jerk wrong. After months of grueling training, when the thought of proving that guy wrong pushed me through some long, lonely runs, he was the first person I thought of as I crossed the finish line in my first marathon.

The completion of that goal of running a marathon provided me with one of the most euphoric moments I can recall. It was all made possible by setting a series of goals, as well as lots of positive and negative motivation, that kept driving me to run and train, especially when I wanted to give up and say that I had had enough.

As I said earlier in this piece, I have since completed nearly fifty marathons and ultra-marathons (anything longer than twenty-six miles). When I first started running from park bench to park bench if you had told me that I would run one ultra-marathon, let alone eight, I would have called you crazy. But I learned some very valuable lessons from my running. I learned that you can accomplish just about anything if you set it as a goal and are willing to do the work necessary to get there. I also learned that life, like running, is about setting a pace for yourself. You run, or live, at a pace that makes sense for you. If you try to run too fast, you risk getting too tired and dropping out of the race. If you run too slow, you risk getting bored and losing interest. You need to find a comfortable pace that will allow you to stay in the race and be competitive for the long haul. Running, and life, is simply putting one foot in front of the other as you traverse the course.

At my first ultra-marathon, I also learned that I can do anything for a day. As I stood in the dark at the starting line thinking about the one hundred-kilometer (sixty-two-mile) course ahead of me, my first thought was: *Are you crazy?* However, I knew that I only had to put forth the effort for that one day. I didn't run a long race the day before, and I certainly was not going to run a long race the next, so I could go out, do my best, and enjoy the day. The accomplishment of completing that race gave me the confidence and self-esteem to set many other goals in every area of my life.

If you don't set goals, you have nothing to strive toward. And, just as important, you will not have a standard to help you determine when you have arrived at your destination, or where you want to be either personally or organizationally. Goals can be set around career objectives, family or relationship objectives, health or fitness objectives, educational objectives, or for organizations, around sales growth, employee development, quality improvement, new product or idea development, etc. It is important, however, that these goals are measurable. It is helpful to assign some quantifiable measure to your goal, as the specificity of your objective will help you see incremental progress while you move through the process of achieving that goal. If your goals are measurable, you will have a clearer view of what is expected if you are to achieve the specific outcome. The more specific the goal, the more specific your commitment to it will be.

Think about the goals you have set in your personal or organizational life. To date, how successful have you been in achieving them?

Hasn't having specific goals helped you to remain focused on what you want to accomplish and what you need to do to get there? Think about the goals you want to achieve right now in your personal or organizational life. How will they keep you focused and on track through the difficult times of this change process?

List of Goals

_____

_____

_____

_____

_____

_____

_____

_____

_____

CHAPTER FIVE

OBSTACLES

"If you find a path with no obstacles, it probably doesn't lead anywhere."

FRANK A. CLARK

By definition, your environment is very simply your surroundings. The universe is the environment for the earth, as your planet exists within the confines of the universe. The earth is the environment for North America, as your continent exists within the confines of the earth. North America is the environment for the United States, as your country exists within the confines of North America. The United States is the environment for your state, as your state exists within the confines of the United States. Your state is the environment for your town, as your town exists within the confines of your state. Your town is the environment for your neighborhood, as your neighborhood exists within the confines of your town. Your neighborhood is the environment for your home, as your home exists within the confines of your neighborhood.

We all operate within many different environments. Your environment may be physical, such as the world, your town, your home, etc. Your environment may also be social, such as your family, your circle of friends, your associates, etc. Your environment may be organizational, such as your employer, your school, a political party, etc. Your environment may be spiritual, such as a religious community, a common belief system, a common philosophy, etc. Your environment may be experiential, such as your level of intelligence, your level of education, your level of mental challenge or stress, etc. Your environment may be emotional, such as your current level of emotion, how you express or do not express your emotions, etc. Environments can take many forms and shapes, but they are all systematic in that they surround some thought, belief, or activity that you are involved in.

If you are going to assess your current situation, it is important for you to be aware of the environment in which you are attempting to manage or achieve change. Your environment can have a lot to do with whether or not your change effort will be successful. If the environment presents the opportunity for change, then the process may be easier. If the environment presents many threats, the process may be more difficult. For this reason, it is important that you are able to identify and assess the state and nature of your environment.

Think about your environment and how it impacts your life. The weather, for example, can have a definite impact on your life. It always seems easier to have a bright and positive outlook on a sunny day than it does on a cloudy day. If you want to start a regular program of exercise by walking a mile outdoors every day, it is usually easier to begin such a program in the summer than it is in the winter. If your business is selling snow blowers, you generally do better in severe winters than in milder seasons. Insurance agents generally write more disaster policies after serious tornadoes than they do in calm weather. Think about your environment and the effect it has had on your life or the life of your organization.

There are many factors that influence your environment. These outside forces can place a great deal of pressure on your environment and effect how you operate within it. These factors can include:

- economic forces such as the economy, unemployment, inflation, or the like;
- political or social forces such as your current form of federal, state, or local government;
- current social trends;
- cultural forces such as cultural values and habits within your environment or community.

Quite often there is nothing within your power that you can do to alter these forces. It is important to be aware of how they affect you and your environment. Your environment is an important part of your system, and the better you understand it, the better prepared you will be to operate within it.

Input is one of those funny little words that means exactly what it says. Input is something that is put in. In the case of change, it represents what it is that you are going to add or introduce to the change process. It can include your present knowledge, skills, or experience. It can also include the negative side of the equation—your ignorance in certain areas, your lack of skill, or your naiveté in certain issues. Back on the positive side, it can include your willingness to put in effort to work the process, or conversely it can be your ability to procrastinate. Input is a combination of the reality of the traits, characteristics, and abilities that you bring to the change process as well as your ambition or willingness. In essence, it represents what you bring to the table, so to speak, in the process of change.

In assessing the input that is necessary for change, it is important that you realistically look at where you are right now and where you will need to be if the change process is to be successful. You will need to assess your skills, knowledge, experience, desire, willingness, and overall effort level, and then assess if it is sufficient for successful change. If it is not, it will be necessary for you to find a way to make up for your shortcomings or revise your ultimate goal.

Another input that you will need to assess honestly is your expectation for the output of the change process. Just like input is what you put into the process, output is what you take out of the process, or the results.

We all have expectations; it is difficult not to. This is especially true when you are at the point where you are preparing to make a major effort to change some element of your life, or the life of your organization. It is difficult not to have your expectations set extremely high. Usually, expectations are in direct relation to the level of risk. It is important to look honestly at your current level of expectation and make sure that it is realistic. For example, when I first started to get the idea in my head that I wanted to run a marathon, I would fantasize about running the Boston Marathon, one of the most famous and prestigious races in the world. Because so many people want to run this race, they have strict qualifying times. At the time that I started running, the qualifying time for my age group was two hours and thirty minutes. There was no way at the time that I would be able to qualify because of my running ability. There were many marathons that did not have rigid qualifying times. So, although my running the Boston Marathon was unrealistic, there were many other races in which to participate. In over forty years of running, I have never participated in the Boston Marathon; however, I have successfully completed nearly fifty other marathons and ultra-marathons.

We all bring assets and liabilities into any situation. It is important that you are honest with yourself and state exactly what those assets and liabilities are. None of us want to admit to our flaws or those characteristics that are not quite the way we would like them to be. If you are going to be successful in the process of change, however, it is important that you are painfully honest with yourself. Fortunately, I have found that when I am totally honest with myself, my self-perception of my negative qualities is usually not as bad as I imagined. I have found that my positive qualities vastly outweigh my negative ones. This is an opportunity for you to assess where you stand prior to embarking on the change process. In doing so, you will be better prepared to build on your strengths and compensate for your weaknesses. It is better to know where you stand before entering any given situation than to be disappointed once the process is underway.

One input that is critical in the process of making change is desire. If you do not have the desire to change, you will not. The process of change will force you to approach situations differently than you have ever faced them before. If you had approached these situations correctly in the first place, there would really be no reason for you to make a change now. If you do not have the desire to do whatever it takes to make a successful transition, then the end result will be futile, and you may as well quit right now.

Take a few minutes and give some serious thought to exactly what your input is, and can be, in the process of change. Remember that you want to look at both your positive and negative contributions to the change process.

In thinking about change, it is important to look at the barriers that get in the way when going through transition. For me, far and away, the biggest barrier is fear—fear of the unknown, fear of failure, fear of success, fear of being foolish, and fear of being inadequate. I could go on listing the various fears that halt people dead in their tracks and keep them from making a commitment to change. There are two elements that I know help me eliminate fear in my life: faith and experience. You must have faith before you can have experience. Throughout time, all of the great religions have taught us that work without faith is futile. In the case of change, however, that thought might be modified to read that change without faith is impossible.

Many people get hung up here because they don't know what they believe in. It is not important what you believe in, but it is important that you believe in something. It is the strength of your belief, or your faith, that will enable you to successfully make change. Your source of belief be it God, the cosmos, karma, yourself, your organization, your friends, or even the process of change is not important. It is critical that you believe that something outside of your own power will help you take the steps necessary to change your current situation. When you are stuck in such a painful place, unable to change your situation, the last thing you are going to believe is that you can affect change yourself. If you could believe in yourself, you wouldn't be in that place to begin with. That is why it is important for you to put your faith elsewhere, in someone or something that is more powerful than yourself at that given time. You must have faith that there is a source where you can get the strength, knowledge, and help to make the changes you desire.

It is important for you to realize that you are not alone. Isolation is a terrible thing, especially when you are trying to overcome some obstacle. Can you remember back to your first day of school when you were a child? What a fearful situation. You had to leave the safety of your home and go to this strange place, where you were going to spend the day with this strange person called a teacher. If you're like most people, your mother probably took you by the hand and walked you into school that first day and made it a lot easier to face that fear. She assured you that everything would be OK and that she would be waiting for you at the end of the school day. Your mother may have even stayed with you in class for the first few minutes until you were comfortable.

So it is with any change you must make in your life or organization. You need to find the greater force that has the strength or the power to help you overcome your fears and face the obstacle or change that has been having such a negative influence in your life. It is here where you break through the state of isolation or loneliness and realize that you have at your disposal the necessary help and support to face what troubles you most.

Change has always been a good thing for me. I have not always been happy when experiencing the change process. Even though the end result has always been positive and a better place than where I started, I still resist change. I get into an insane frame of mind where I say, *I can't do this! I don't want to change!* I want to avoid the pain of change so badly that I am willing to forfeit the positive results. I hate it when I get this crazy thinking, but sometimes it is unavoidable.

You may be reading this and saying to yourself, "There is no way that I am exhibiting insane behavior!" Think about this for a moment. *Webster's Dictionary*, in addition to defining insanity as a mental disorder, describes it as "something utterly foolish or unreasonable." By this definition, if you really think about your emotional state when you are facing changes in your life, can you say that you do not have a mental disorder? Your thoughts about the current situation in your life or your thoughts and fears are they not *utterly foolish* or *unreasonable*? I don't know about you, but when I am in this state, I need help outside of myself to restore some clarity to my thinking and my actions. When I can put my faith and belief into something or someone who has a better perspective on the situation than I do, it releases me from my fear and gives me the relief and the strength to go about the process of making change. All the success I have had consulting with individuals and organizations is not because of my superior intellect and experience. It is a combination of my knowledge and experience plus a large dose of objectivity that I bring into these situations. I am not intimately involved in the system, and as an objective outsider I am able to see things that those directly involved cannot. Have you ever written a term paper or article and spent hours looking for typos without finding a single one, only to have an objective eye find the three you missed within seconds?

Another way to look at this situation is that insanity is the absence of reality, and conversely sanity is the acceptance of reality. In this process, we need to accept reality and not let its absence be a barrier to our ability to change.

Developing hope that things will get better and making the commitment to follow through on the process can be made a lot easier when you can see the benefits you will realize as a result of change. It helps to develop the optimism, excitement, and commitment needed to get started on the change process.

In coming to grips with some of the fears keeping you from making successful change and finding the source in which to place your trust and faith, it would be helpful to ask yourself the following questions:

- **What is your fear like, and how does it affect your life and/ or your organization?**

- **In what specific events or occurrences has fear affected your life, and what were the ensuing consequences?**

- **How has your fear affected others, and what consequences has it introduced into their lives and/or organizations?**

- What people or resource can help you overcome your fears and affect change?

  _____

  _____

- What are the positive benefits of making changes in your life and/or organization?

  _____

  _____

- What are the barriers standing in the way of you successfully making change?

  _____

  _____

It is important to draw a distinction between shame and guilt. *Webster's Dictionary* defines shame as "a painful sense of having done something wrong, improper, or immodest." Guilt is a feeling of responsibility for your offensive behavior. You can be responsible for your behavior, make amends to the offended party, and thus deal with the guilt. Shame, unfortunately, is directed inwards. It is often a feeling that results from, or that you feel in conjunction with, guilt over your behavior. Shame can be either healthy or unhealthy depending on where it originates and how you use it. Healthy shame causes you to rectify any offensive situation and alter the behavior. The shame and guilt are then released. Unhealthy shame is oppressive and causes you to chastise yourself for being less than perfect, defective, evil, or any number of self-destructive or demeaning feelings or attitudes. In essence, you tell yourself that you are worthless.

In his extensive writings on shame, John Bradshaw (1998) talks about dysfunctional family systems and how shame is often a factor that keeps everyone in line. In a family situation where the parents are *shame-less*, the child in the family has no option but to accept the shame for their parents because they will never accept responsibility for their own behavior. These children tell themselves that they are somehow flawed and accept all blame, responsibility, and shame for all that goes wrong in their surroundings. If your parents have no shame, it is natural to conclude that you must be the one who is, or must be, shameful.

In the family system that I grew up in, my parents were the ultimate authority on everything and could do no wrong. The rule of thumb in my family was:

- **Rule #1: Your parents are always right!**
- **Rule #2: When your parents are wrong, refer to Rule #1!**

Consequently, in my family system no matter what I did, the possibility always existed that I would be proven wrong. Naturally, I did not grow up very sure of myself, and I learned to always question anything I did. I strove for perfection, for perfection was the only way to avoid the shame that went along with displeasing my parents. A standard line in my family was "that's ok, but you can always do better." Thus, my best was never good enough and that provided me with two options. One, always keep trying to do better at everything you do with the ultimate goal of being perfect, knowing that you will never really get there. Or, two, accept the fact that you will never get it right and give up. I found myself alternating back and forth between the two options.

I was naturally quite confused. Sometimes, when I caught my parents in a good mood and got their approval, I felt on top of the world. On other days, when their mood was not so pleasant, and they were in the mood for finding fault or passing on their own sense of shame at their own failings, I felt completely worthless. It was a no-win situation.

Unfortunately, the lessons you learn early in life do not automatically go away when you become an adult. Throughout my life I have always questioned everything I have done, asking myself things like *is it good enough, will they like what I have done, will I get the recognition and approval I so desperately seek.* It takes a lot of effort to get to the point where you realize that you are the only one who can truly approve of or adequately judge your own efforts. A person who is shame-based seeks approval from outside of themselves because by themselves they are quite often wrong, improper, or immodest in their behavior. At least, that's how they perceive things.

Shame can be a huge barrier to making change. It triggers all of our fears and can either make us super achievers or keep us immobilized in inactivity. When you live with the fear that you are worthless and that your efforts will never be good enough, you often become an over-achiever who believes you have to be better than everyone else to be OK. Or, you may revert to the state where you wonder why you should try at all. If you reach this stage, you have lost. You need to change those internal messages that say you are worthless and replace them with messages that reinforce your true worth as a person.

We all have worth. Every day that you are alive you interact with others, and you have a definite impact on the lives of those people. If you have children, where would they be without you? How would your company or business operate if you did not show up when you were scheduled to work? If you play on any sports team, what would happen if you did not show up for a game? In the movie *It's a Wonderful Life* (1945), the character George Bailey was feeling pretty worthless and was so overwhelmed by his problems that he wished he had never been born. He was allowed the unique opportunity to see just what would have happened if he had not been born and how so many lives would have been impacted if he had not been around to make his important contribution to the world. The same is true for you. By your very existence you take up an important space in the universe, and how you decide to live will have long-standing consequences not only on your life, but on the lives of the people you encounter on a daily basis. That in itself means you are pretty important. That's why it is critical that you find your true sense of worth. It is difficult to do, but it is necessary if you are to make effective change in your personal or organizational life.

The only true counter to shame is self-esteem. The higher you perceive yourself, your self-esteem, the lower the chance of being crippled by shame. It is important to get an accurate picture of yourself and your true worth as an individual or an organization. Think about a time when you were not feeling very good about yourself. How easy was it to get motivated to go out and do something positive for yourself or others? Perhaps you had a hard time getting out of bed, getting started on a project, or wanting to participate in an activity with your family or friends. Then think about a time when you were really feeling good about yourself and your ability to accomplish your goals. You were probably pretty motivated and were eager to continue to do positive things for yourself. Self-esteem can be the motivating factor that is the difference between success and failure. If you don't feel very good about yourself or your organization, you probably won't go too far out of your way to change. If, on the other hand, you really feel good about yourself or your organization, you will want to experience the excitement and positive benefits of change and will pursue it aggressively.

Think about the impact of shame in your life and how you can eliminate the barrier to effective change. Some questions to consider when thinking about the unhealthy shame in your life or organization include:

- **What were some of the messages you have received in your life that had a shaming effect on you?**

  _____

  _____

  _____

  _____

- **How have these messages affected your behavior today?**

  _____

  _____

- **How have these shaming messages acted as barriers to keep you from affecting positive change?**

  _____

  _____

- How can you counter these messages?

  _____

  _____

- What are some positive messages you can give yourself to replace these negative messages?

  _____

  _____

- What are some things you can do on a regular basis to build your self-esteem?

  _____

  _____

Stress is a part of your everyday life. In the strictest definition of the word, it is a pressure or strain that tends to distort the body. Your body is stressed by the force of gravity. It is stressed by the pressure of the fluids on your inside pushing out and the force of air on the outside pushing in. These are natural stresses necessary to sustain life as you know it. These are normal and healthy stressors.

There are abnormal and unhealthy stressors as well. These stressors can induce physical or mental pressure. Such stressors can include overwork and fatigue, fear or hate, exposure or injury, hurry and tension, expectations or pressures—virtually anything that forces you to operate at a state greater than that in which you are comfortable operating, or which is not normal for you.

An interesting thing happens to you when you are exposed to stress. Your body produces a fight reaction, or what is called Generalized Adaption Syndrome. When an outside pressure threatens you, the body rushes to supply protection for itself by turning on its chemical "juices" and preparing to defend itself. The brain senses pressure from an external or internal stimulus. It then sends a message to the hypothalamus, pituitary gland, and autonomic nervous system. Adrenaline

floods nerve endings, blood pressure rises, blood clotting time is re-
duced, sugar is pumped to fuel muscles, and cholesterol and fats are
mobilized in the bloodstream. It is precisely for this reason that under
undue pressure people have been known to exhibit abnormal feats of
strength, speed, or endurance. The body protects itself from the stressors, which help the body to perform at unnatural levels. Unfortunately,
if it is asked time and time again to react to pressure and continually
fight against stressors, the body finally produces exhaustion. When it
can no longer gear itself up to fight, it begins to break down with grad-
ual damaging effects on the circulatory system and lungs, the digestive
system, the muscles and joints, not to mention damage to mental and
emotional health. Prolonged exposure to this process can result in dis-
ease, including arthritis, emotional disorders, and cardiovascular and
gastrointestinal conditions. It also hastens the aging process.

There are three basic stages of stress. The first is the alarm stage,
where you become concerned about a situation or event. During this
stage, you may experience symptoms like restlessness, anxiety, anger,
depression, or fear. The second stage is the resistance stage, where you
begin to fight the consequences of the situation or event. Symptoms
include denial of feelings, emotional isolation, or narrowing of interests. The final stage is the exhaustion stage, where you begin to experience the serious consequences of stress. Symptoms of this stage include loss of self-confidence, loss of sleep, unusual and erratic behavior,
and finally physical or emotional disorders.

Think about a time when you were stressed out at home, at work,
or perhaps in a social situation. At first your palms became sweaty, and
you felt a little jittery. You tried telling yourself that it was nothing and
that you could tough your way through any situation. Then by the end
of the day when you got home, you were so exhausted that you just
collapsed into bed because you had no energy left to do anything else.
This is stress and the effect it can have on us.

THE EFFECTS OF STRESS

STRESSORS

Overwork & Fatigue
Fear & Hate
Exposure & Injury
Hurry & Tension
Expectations & Pressures

STRESS

Generalized Adaptation Syndrome
The Fight Reaction

DIS-EASE

Arthritis
Emotional Disorders
Cardiovascular
Gastrointestinal

THE STAGES OF STRESS

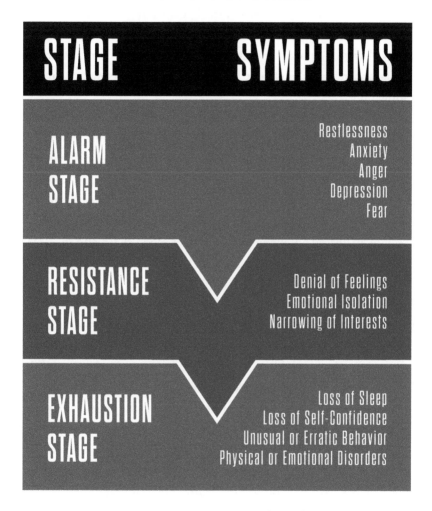

STAGE	SYMPTOMS
ALARM STAGE	Restlessness Anxiety Anger Depression Fear
RESISTANCE STAGE	Denial of Feelings Emotional Isolation Narrowing of Interests
EXHAUSTION STAGE	Loss of Sleep Loss of Self-Confidence Unusual or Erratic Behavior Physical or Emotional Disorders

By its very nature, the change process produces a great deal of stress. You put an enormous amount of pressure on yourself to get through the change process quickly, to do it perfectly, and to accomplish it easily. Sometimes you take on or assume the expectations of others or you let your unhealthy shame dictate how you should perform. Often your spouse or significant other, your family, your friends, your associates, or your organization provide outside pressure, which produces stress.

The fear that you often experience in the change process also produces a great deal of pressure, which can add stress to your life. No matter where it comes from, or what form it comes in, stress can act as a barrier to reaching your desired state of change. It is important that you deal with it quickly and effectively if you are to eliminate it as a barrier and realize the change you desire in your personal or organizational life.

The first place to start when dealing with stress is to recognize exactly what produces it in your life or organization and just how it affects you. Quite often you dismiss stress and treat it as a normal everyday occurrence. Stress may occur in your life every day; however, it is far from normal. Most likely you just get used to the pressure, and your body gets used to operating in a fighting mode with higher blood pressure, increased adrenaline levels, higher blood sugar, and increased cholesterol levels. This is not a normal way to operate. If you keep forcing yourself to operate at this high level of stress, it will not be long before you become sick, depressed, or exhausted. You need to identify the stress in your life and learn how to deal with it. If you doubt this, look at the concerns about obesity, the advertising for cholesterol-lowering medication, high blood pressure and hypertension levels, and the rate of depression that is prevalent in the United States today.

There are a number of ways to deal with stress. The easiest, and probably the most effective, way is to simply talk about it. Unfortunately, you often tell yourself that you can't do that because it wouldn't be appropriate, or that your spouse or friends will get sick of hearing about your problems, or that you need to learn how to tough it out. The fact is things happen in your daily life that sometimes confuse you, frighten you, threaten you, or simply throw you for a loop. Many of these occurrences are normal learning experiences; however, for many of us these are first-time experiences. It is perfectly normal and appropriate for you to question the situation, turn to another for advice, or talk about it to hear yourself verbalize the situation and your experience, and get it off your chest. The process of talking about a difficult situation or experience can very often eliminate most of the stress.

You can also take other actions to help reduce the stress in your life. Meditation is a form of relaxation that helps clear your mind of the thoughts that act as stressors. Physical exercise is a great way to relax, unwind, and clear your mind as well as build up your body's ability to counter the physical effects of stress. Simply getting away from the situation or event can serve as a way to put some distance between you and the stressors until you are ready to deal directly with the issue.

Ultimately, the clearest and most long-lasting way to handle stress is to deal directly with the issue at hand. If you can incorporate some or all of the techniques discussed above, it will be easier to move through the stressful period and into the new state of change you desire.

All change involves loss. When you change a behavior, you must give up those behaviors that served you so well and loyally in the past. If you change careers, you must give up the profession that has occupied so much of your time and energy. If you change jobs, you must give up the daily companionship of your co-workers and the security and traditions that have been so familiar and comfortable. If you end a relationship, you must give up the dependence you have placed upon that person for friendship, love, affection, or support that has been so important to you in that relationship. Even if the relationship was painful or destructive, if the job was killing you, or if the career was going nowhere, the loss is real and must be grieved.

Grief is inescapable in life. You must grieve, and if you don't, you carry the pain of your losses with you. It is not uncommon for people to carry losses with them for years only to have their grief surface during the most unlikely time or circumstance. My father died when I was in my early twenties. At the time of his death, I was incapable of fully grieving my loss, mainly because I did not fully understand it. I had patterned my life after my father's; he was my hero after all. I acted the way he acted. I dressed the way he dressed. I ate the way he ate. I thought the way he thought. I even chose the same career that he chose. I was living my father's life. I was a living, breathing clone of my father, even though that was the last thing in the world I wanted to be. My father was the ultimate authority in my life. He was the ultimate source of my self-worth as I constantly sought his approval.

He was bigger than life and, in my eyes, invincible. And then at the age of fifty-four he was gone. I was shattered. How could such a powerful man succumb to disease?

It wasn't until years later, after drifting aimlessly in search of a role model, that I was faced with a life-shifting traumatic situation that forced me to fully realize the extent of my loss. When my father died, a big part of me died as well. All I knew how to be was what I saw my father be. I thought that this man was indestructible and that he would live forever. And then he died, and so did the part of me that was just like him. It wasn't until I was fully able to accept that my loss went beyond my father's death and that I needed to grieve this loss fully, that I was able to move past it and discover what my life truly meant to me and how I wanted to live it. The result of the grief work was the ability to begin making good decisions about what I wanted my life to be and to begin a new relationship with myself. I changed my lifestyle to one that better suited the new me. I changed how I took care of myself. I discovered some values that were important to me. I even changed careers and chose one that was important to me and my values rather than one that my father would approve of. It was the grieving of my father's death that gave me the freedom to let go of the past and face my future.

Elizabeth Kübler-Ross (1969), in her book *On Death and Dying*, identified five stages in the grief process:

- Shock or Denial: At first, you don't believe what is happening to you with your loss, or you refuse to accept it. The loss is so great that you just don't want to admit it. Many of us simply don't want to go through the pain, so we avoid admitting we have suffered any loss.

- Anger and Depression: Not many people take losses gracefully; they get upset and angry at losing anything. Many people repress this anger, and when they do the result is depression. In any event, it is important to get this anger out before it becomes destructive to you or others.

- Bargaining: When you lose something, you will attempt to make deals to get it back. How many times as a child did you try to strike a deal with your parents that if they let you stay up late this one time, you would be good forever?

- Disappointment or Depression: There are not too many people who are not disappointed when they lose something. Disappointment is a natural part of loss and should not be denied.

- Acceptance and Integration: Finally, in the process of grief, you have no alternative but to accept the loss and resulting change and integrate it into your life. This part may take time, but eventually it will happen.

When going through the grief process, it is important that you go through each of these stages. Some will take longer than others. You may need to go through certain stages more than once. You may often feel like you are backsliding. It is important, however, to remember that what helps in the grieving process more than anything else is time. Time, as the saying goes, heals all wounds. It is critical for you to give yourself time to grieve your losses, and it is just as important for you to give yourself permission to feel the loss. I know in many instances my first reaction to a loss is to tell myself that I cannot feel the pain of loss, and that I should be *bigger* or *stronger* than that. But the reality of life is that it sometimes hurts. When I don't get that job I really want, it is disappointing. When I am interested in a woman but she is not interested in me, it hurts. When I make my presentation to go after a new piece of business but they decide to use someone else, it is painful. I must grieve these losses before I can move on. And that takes time. I also usually try to rush the process. I tell myself that I must get through this quickly and get on with my life. I have found if I rush the process, though, I will just have to re-experience that loss and grieve it later.

One of the biggest mistakes you can make in the grief process is to try to go through it all by yourself. Yes, you, and only you, can experience the grief, but that does not mean you cannot utilize people and other resources to help you get through the grief. A spouse or loved one, a friend, a co-worker, a counselor, a support group, or a religious or spiritual community can be a great comfort and assistance in this process. Sometimes knowing that you are not doing this all by yourself can make the process easier. It is often valuable and helpful just to talk about what you are experiencing to better understand it and how you are processing the experience.

Generally, as you go through life, somewhere along the line your behavior or actions will cause harm. You may also leave these actions or behaviors unresolved—your unfinished business. It may have been something you said, some mistake you made, or some injustice you overlooked as you struggled to get where you thought you wanted to be. It could be a project you attempted and never finished, or simply an appointment or date you never kept. It is imperative if you are to make changes in your life that you take responsibility for those actions and be willing to rectify the situation. You must be willing to resolve your unfinished business.

You may ask yourself, "How can I recall all of the situations or issues that I left unresolved? How do I know all the people or organizations I have injured in my lifetime? Besides, it's probably no big deal." I know for me there were times when I had unresolved issues, which acted as barriers, keeping me from getting where I wanted to be because I was either too afraid or too uncomfortable with the thought of dealing with the people or situation involved. I know immediately when I am in one of those situations because I have the habit of talking to myself out loud when I am embarrassed or uncomfortable. It is almost as if I am trying to scare away those embarrassing thoughts that get locked in my head. It doesn't matter how old the experiences may be, the response is always the same until I resolve them.

When faced with an embarrassing or unresolved issue, some people will avoid people, places, or situations where they may be forced to face that unresolved issue. How many times in your life have you had an unresolved issue with someone and then when you see them coming your way, you quickly turn around, avert your eyes, walk on the other side of the street, or take some other tact rather than face the fear or the embarrassment, or even just an uncomfortable feeling. The only way you can truly escape these thoughts is to get them out and resolve them once and for all.

Rectifying or amending the situation involves more than merely saying I'm sorry. That's very easy to do, and many of us have used that as an excuse for continuing the behavior. Does this sound familiar? "I said I'm sorry. What else do they want? Besides, it's no big deal!"

I don't know how many times in my life I have been sorry for something I have done and quickly used the words *I'm sorry* as a means to escape any serious consequence. I was usually quick to repeat the offending behavior unless I made some effort to change my viewpoint, understanding, or attitude that brought about my inappropriate behavior in the first place. Webster's defines the word amend as "to put right; to change or modify for the better: improve; to reform oneself." Nowhere in this definition does it say anything about being sorry. In fact, an apology without an accompanying changed behavior can be a bigger insult than the original indiscretion.

In rectifying any behavior, or in making any change, there is an old saying that is very appropriate: "Charity begins at home." In a situation where you are unable to bring about a change, the person your behavior generally hurts the most is you. If you are to successfully go out and make restitution to others for your behavior, you must first come to grips with what you have done to yourself. I recently heard dysfunction described as a set of behaviors, beliefs, actions, or feelings that are self-destructive; the only cure for dysfunction is self-esteem. Feeling good about yourself and your actions, or positive self-esteem, will make it much easier to go out and change the behavior you deem unacceptable, especially in an instance where the behavior has hurt others. If you are successful at seeing how new changes can positively affect your life, it will encourage you even more to practice the principle with others. I know how much satisfaction and self-esteem I realize from completing something that I have started. It is just much more rewarding to resolve some issue that I have left hanging for some time.

In a long running comic strip, *The Family Circus* (1993) by Bil Keane, the characters Jeffy and Dolly are constantly being victimized by "Ida Know" and "Not Me," spirits who cause all kinds of mischief. It is amazing how easy it is for us to shift blame to something or someone else. This way you never have to take responsibility for your

actions. It seems, however, that everyone but us is aware of our behavior, and sooner or later, everyone will stop allowing us to get away
with it or will have nothing to do with us. If you are to overcome the
obstacles keeping you from making changes, you must be willing to
change the behavior that got you into the situation you are in and to
right any wrongs you may have caused in the process.

If you can change your behavior and resolve old wounds or disagreements from your past, you can successfully eliminate the barriers
blocking you from realizing your goals. Once and for all, you can be
free of those nagging feelings, which often reside deep in your subconscious and are often the root of many self-defeating messages that
you give yourself. If you can eliminate the source of the dis-ease, you
can eliminate many of the limiting messages you give yourself or your
organization.

You can begin this process by making a list of the situations, people,
or organizations where you have unfinished business and determining
how and when you can amend or rectify the situation. Then comes an
even more difficult part of the process, you must find a way to resolve
the situation without causing any further harm. When attempting to
make restitution for a past indiscretion or unresolved issue, you must
be mindful of anything that could make this situation worse than it already may be. If a direct approach will cause even more hurt and pain,
you must determine if this is a wise approach to rectify the situation.

You may also have some unfinished business in your work world.
You may have a past indiscretion with a co-worker or customer that
was never resolved that might resurface at the most inappropriate time.
Unresolved issues at work often evolve into personality or turf battles,
which can prevent the organization from reaching its full potential. A
dispute with a customer can result in lost business or even a tarnished
reputation within the industry. No matter how scary or painful these
situations may be, it is in the best interests of the organization to get
them resolved.

There are many barriers that keep you from achieving the change
you desire. Many of these barriers are real situations or issues, which
prevent you from moving further along your desired path.

One of the barriers that can get in the way of your making change is education. Lack of a proper education has stopped many people dead in their tracks in their quest to better their lives. Poverty and lack of education are synonymous. Research has shown that in many cases income rises in direct correlation with your level of education. Lack of a formal education can often keep you from reaching the goals you strive for. For example, I have always had this vision that I would work for a large corporation, own my own business, and someday retire and teach at some small college. My college undergraduate degree served me well in reaching the first two goals; however, I found it more difficult to realize the third without at least a master's degree. Colleges and universities put a great deal of stock in the degrees a person has earned because it is important for them to line up the most prestigious and qualified faculty possible as they compete for students. It was ironic that seventeen years after I received my baccalaureate degree, I was back at school pursuing my master's degree. If I wanted to continue to teach at the college level, it was essential that I continue my education. My ambition and desire to grow in my career as an academic administrator dictated that I earn a doctorate, which I did after I completed my master's studies. Learning is a lifelong need, and I continue to learn the formal and informal lessons necessary for my success.

Not all education must lead to a degree. I worked with a friend who was trying to decide what he wanted to be when he grew up, just as most of us do all of our lives. He had enjoyed a long and successful career in the restaurant field, having managed many popular restaurants. Due to a disagreement with the owner, he left his last position and began to review his options. He knew he would have no difficulty landing a position managing a restaurant for someone else, but he did not know if that was what he really wanted to do. He also considered opening his own restaurant, but he did not know if he could secure financing in the prevailing economy nor was he sure if he was ready to make the step. He had always been a very good amateur cook although he had never really had any formal training as a chef. He thought he knew what he was doing with regards to cooking; however, due to his lack of a formal education, he was not sure. He looked at his situation;

he was single, free of debt, and ideally suited to go back to school, so he decided it was the time. By attending cooking school, he could eliminate a barrier to successful change by gaining the formal training he lacked. Regardless of which direction he chose upon completion, he would be a more complete person both in his knowledge and in his confidence.

Education is not the only barrier that holds people back. Very often experience, or lack of it, keeps people from realizing their goal of achieving meaningful change. In many situations, experience can be more valuable than education. There are many successful entrepreneurs, for example, who never graduated from high school. Bill Gates left Harvard University without graduating to begin Microsoft, and Mark Zuckerberg left Harvard to launch Facebook. The education they received through their experiences in the real world more than compensated for what they did not learn in the classroom.

People often underestimate the value of their experience. I know that many of the people I have worked with over the years, in both my personal and business consulting, have underestimated the value of their life experiences. Many women drop out of the workforce for some time to raise their children. I have found that a lot of them want to return to work after their children reach school age. In fact, many of them have the dream of running their own business, but they believe that they lack the experience to do so. When you really think about it, however, running a household is a lot like running a company. You have to manage the household budget, coordinate and orchestrate all of the activities of the people living within the house; make sure all of the household chores and responsibilities are complete; plan and prepare meals, manage and care for the home; clean clothes; get children to school; make sure homework is done; and get everyone to sports, clubs, doctors, dentists, etc. It takes a pretty skilled manager to keep a household running smoothly.

There may be other barriers that can get in the way of achieving a desired change. Physical barriers may prevent you from completing all the actions necessary to achieve a change. I have worked with people with medical conditions, such as heart disease, which prevented them from doing strenuous activities. One businessperson I worked with could not make many daily sales calls because it was too physically taxing. This was a serious barrier in promoting his business. In order for this person to reach his goal of growing his business, he realized that it would be necessary for him to hire a salesperson to do the work he was not able to do.

Emotional situations may also be a barrier. Many people are not emotionally secure enough to deal with stressful change, and it is necessary for them to seek emotional support, or in some cases psychological care, before embarking on a serious change process.

Financial problems are often a barrier to successful change. Many people would like to go back to school, or change jobs, or move; however, past debt or low savings prevent them from doing it right away. Hundreds of small businesses fail or never get started each year because the owner cannot secure the necessary funding.

No matter what the barrier may be, there is usually a way to overcome it. The solution may not always be simple or quick, but it is there. It is important not to get discouraged when looking at these barriers. Try to keep things in perspective. When I first started graduate school, I thought it would take forever to finish my degree just taking one course at a time. But before I knew it, four years had passed, and I was finished. If you concentrate on what you can do right now instead of being overwhelmed by the enormity of the barrier, it will seem a lot more manageable and possible to overcome.

CHAPTER SIX

RESOURCES

"All the resources you need are in the mind."

THEODORE ROOSEVELT

O ne of the most difficult things for us to do individually, or as an organization, is to step back and take an honest look at ourselves. No one wants to admit that they are imperfect or expose their blemishes. If you are to make all the changes you want to in life, it is essential to take a long, hard look at yourself or your organization and inventory your strengths and weaknesses.

Any good business knows that it is important to take a regular inventory. Quite simply, an inventory lets the business take stock of its assets. It lets them know what they have on hand and what they don't. An inventory gives them important information needed to plan for the operation and growth of their business, such as what items are selling and what aren't, what raw materials they have in stock and what needs to be reordered, or what the value of their physical assets is. All of this information is used to determine the value or worth of the company.

You can take this concept and use it in your organization or apply it to your personal life. An inventory can help you determine exactly who you are. And, of course, you need to know who you are before you can determine who you want to be. You can inventory your strengths and weaknesses, the things you like about yourself or your organization and the things you don't. You can look at the things you are proud of and the things you are ashamed about. You can inventory your current skills and those you need to develop, or you can look at your likes and dislikes, the things you enjoy doing and those you don't. You can look at the things you do well and the things you don't. In essence, you need to fully evaluate yourself and look at what you have and what you don't have to determine what you need to change.

It is also important to inventory your value system and personality characteristics. Each of us was born with our own unique personality, and over time developed a set of values that we live our lives by. When you go against your value system, it causes you uneasiness and pain, often resulting in guilt and shame. The more you go against your values and the more guilt and shame you inflict upon yourself, the more your self-esteem suffers and the harder it is for you to make changes. It is important that you define your values to provide yourself with guidelines for the decisions you make and the actions you take in life.

Try as you will there is really no way to change your personality, but you can work to understand it and how it dictates your actions and reactions to others. There are many schools of thought on the different character and temperament types. There are any number of instruments available to help identify psychological differences that drive behavior. One of the most logical and easiest to understand and use was developed by the team of Dr. Isabel Briggs Myers and Dr. Katharine Briggs. Known as the Myers-Briggs Type Indicator (1980), it is a tool for identifying sixteen different patterns of action. This work was further developed by the team of Dr. David Keirsey and Dr. Marilyn Bates (1984). Their theory holds that there are sixteen different character and temperament types based on four pairs of preferred actions. The Keirsey-Bates Character and Temperament Types are broken down into four pairs of preferred action types as follows:

- **Extraversion (social and interactive) vs. Introversion (concentrative and territorial)**

- **Intuition (concerned by the possibilities) vs. Sensation (concerned with the here and now)**

- **Thinking (objective, logical) vs. Feeling (personal, emotional)**

• **Judging (prefer closure, deadlines, planning) vs. Perceiving (prefer to keep options open and fluid)**

Another interesting look at personality can be found in David Marcus and Steven Smith's (2007) book *Egonomics: What Makes Ego Our Greatest Asset (or Most Expensive Liability)*. Marcus and Smith posit that ego, either positive or negative, helps to form your behavior and shape your strengths and weaknesses. A full description of all the theories discussed above can be found in their books listed in the bibliography.

One of the things I have found to be true in life is that I cannot change my basic personality no matter how hard I try. Because of who I am, and the skills and talents that I have been blessed with and have developed, there are certain things I will excel at and others at which I will be a dismal failure. It seems that when I dwell on the things I don't do well, I experience problems. Conversely, if I work on those things I do well, I experience a great deal of success. In general, I'm happier, enjoy those activities more, feel confident, procrastinate less, and usually exert more effort in achieving success in those areas. Experience has taught me that if I concentrate on those behaviors and activities that I do well and either avoid or find a way to compensate for the behaviors or activities that I do not excel at, I will experience more happiness and success in my life.

For example, one of the things I have learned about myself in my work life is that I can go into any situation and very quickly get a clear picture of what is going on in an organization. I can assess their situation and develop a clear idea and a plan of what they need to do to change their present circumstance. I enjoy the variety of situations, organizations, and challenges. I get bored dealing with the same issues day-after-day. I love the discovery, analyzing, and planning part of the process, but I find the implementation stage tedious. For me, the consultative and educational part of the job is where I fully utilize my skills, so I have focused my career on those types of opportunities. I avoid assignments or jobs that require routine repetitive work. When I find an assignment that requires both, I solicit the help of an associate whose skills are on the implementation side of the equation. In this way I am maximizing my strengths and compensating for my weaknesses.

One of the things I have always had trouble doing either on a personal or professional level is saying *no*. People will ask me to get involved in a project, and I will look at the possibilities, get excited, and want to get involved; that is the "Intuitive" in me. The "Judger" in me wants to get the process concluded as quickly as possible so I can move on to the next exciting challenge. As a result, I sometimes make decisions too quickly and find myself involved with situations in which I may not have adequate time or energy to devote to the challenge. Knowing my personality and how I tend to operate has helped me in these situations where I tend to say *yes* too quickly. I have learned to stop, step back, and say, "Let me think about that for a while." Handling the request in this manner allows me time to let the excitement of the offer die down, so I can look more closely at the facts and determine if it is something I really want to be involved in. When I operate in this manner, I am often happier because I make better choices.

In this process of change, it is critical to take adequate stock of yourself or your organization. It is essential to be honest and thorough in your inventory and to remember that you are doing this so you can realize all the changes you desire.

We all have needs that must be met if we are to be successful in life. Some of those needs are more pressing than others. A man walking through the desert needs water, or he will perish. Some of those needs may be taken to an extreme. BASE jumpers have a need for excitement and often put their lives at risk to get their thrills. Some of those needs are denied and never met. Some people are hungry for companionship, but they let their fear of people keep them isolated and away from meeting others who can provide friendship and support. If you are to be successful on your path, it is important to understand and develop a strategy for meeting the needs necessary to achieve successful change.

Psychologist Abraham Maslow (1954) categorized human needs and arranged them in a hierarchy, which describes the different levels of needs humans experience and require. Maslow's hierarchy is illustrated in the following chart.

Maslow identified the lowest level of needs as physiological needs. These include basic needs like food, clothing, shelter, rest, exercise, etc. From a standpoint of change, it is important that your basic needs are being met on a day-to-day basis if you are to be effective in making transitions in your life or organization.

As an example, take the small business owner who opens a new company and with all the problems associated with a start-up phase immediately begins working extra hours. At first it is just an hour or two a day after closing. Then it becomes evenings, then weekends. Sooner or later she will stop eating regular meals, will sit up late at night worrying and not get the proper amount of sleep, or will not get enough exercise. Before you know it, she is sick and cannot work at all, and the business fails because the owner is physically unable to run it. I once worked with a business owner who literally would stay at his shop all night pacing back and forth worrying about his business. Naturally he did not get very much sleep; as a result, he was so tired during the day that he was irritable, could not think clearly and made poor decisions, and could not understand why his business was doing so poorly.

When I was working at a local community college, a student was brought to my attention because she was struggling with her classes. She was causing some difficulty in some of her classes because she was not showing up, and when she did, she would fall asleep. Her lack of cleanliness was also causing distractions for other students. Upon investigation, I found out this young woman was constantly fighting with her mother, who was a single parent (her father was out of the picture). The young woman had moved out of her mother's house and was sleeping in her car, bathing in the college lavatories, and working three part-time jobs to pay for food and gas and to cover her college expenses. Unfortunately, she eventually dropped out of school because she could not focus both on her education and meeting her physiological needs.

The next level of needs according to Maslow are safety needs. We all need to feel safe if we are to function properly. We need to feel safe not only physically, but also mentally, emotionally, financially, and spiritually. Think back to the last time you started a new job. On your first day you probably did not feel completely safe. Quite possibly the only person you knew was the one who hired you. You needed to learn something about the people you would be working with to see if it was safe to open up to them. You needed to assess your immediate surroundings to see if they posed any physical threat to you. You needed to feel comfortable and secure in your work area. You needed to learn something about the work environment to know if it was safe to honestly and candidly say what you were thinking. You needed to find out what the culture of the organization was all about to determine if it had the same values you did. Many of these things you do automatically on a daily basis, often without thinking. If you're going to make a successful change, it is important that you ensure your safety needs are met, especially if the change requires you to take a significant risk.

I can remember a particular instance where I was a little too verbal with my honesty in appraising an issue. I thought I was safe in this employment situation, but I had not evaluated the situation properly. I told my supervisor in a conversation that I was disturbed by the way the organization had positioned itself in working with a major client. I told him that it felt as if we were always battling with the client and were in an adversarial position, like we were always right, and they were always wrong. I told him that it did not feel good working in this us versus them environment. The company would usually preface their advice to the client with a statement like: "When we had the Acme account, we would do it this way!" The client resented being treated like they did not know what they were doing. After I had this conversation with my supervisor where I asked for his guidance, I was positioned as not being a team player and as being unwilling to promote the corporate line of thought. Sometime later when the company was downsizing, I was laid off. The company later lost the account because the client resented the condescending attitude of the company. I, having been relieved to be out of that organization, went on to open and run my own business for the next ten years and had one of the most important periods of change and growth in my life.

After we have met our need for safety, Maslow says that individuals must meet their need for socialization. We all want to belong, and it is important that we feel like we fit in. Have you ever witnessed a child who moves into a new neighborhood and enrolls in a new school? The things that child will go through to make friends and belong to that new community are amazing. They will attempt to belong through their words, actions, appearance, and attitudes. They want to fit in so badly that they will do just about anything to be accepted by the group. In today's world, it is even more difficult because so many of the socialization benchmarks are so expensive. It is important to have the right clothes and the right hair color and cut, to have the right smart phone and above average texting skills, to play the right video games, to attend the coolest concerts ... this list goes on and on. It is ironic how teenagers, in particular, who are trying to exert their independence from their family systems will try to find so much uniformity and conformity to fit into social situations.

If you are going to make any kind of successful change, it is critical to have a sense of belonging with the new environment you are trying to enter. If not, you will never fully be comfortable and may not feel like you have made a successful transition. In many cases, you will return to the place you came from because it is more comfortable, even if you really hate being there. Socialization needs encompass belonging, acceptance, and a sense of family, friendship, love, and affection.

The next level of needs are esteem needs. We all need to feel that we have worth as individuals. Remember that definition of dysfunction I mentioned earlier: "an oppressive set of thoughts, actions, behaviors, or attitudes that are self-destructive." Again, the best cure for dysfunction is self-esteem. It seems so much easier to do anything when you are feeling good about yourself, when you believe yourself to have value, and when you hold yourself in high regard.

I have a close friend who was working for a business that was going through some major reorganization. My friend had been a major player in the company's growth and development throughout its history. He was well liked and respected within the company. A new CEO was hired and began to bring in his own people for top management positions. My friend was overlooked for a promotion for which he was well qualified. Not only was he passed over, but his new boss made promises to him about his title, his responsibilities, his staff, his salary, and even the location of his office, which were never kept. My friend tried to keep up his spirit and his enthusiasm, but he was unhappy in his new work environment, felt disrespected, and ultimately his self-esteem began to suffer. Ultimately, he needed to find a new position with a company who truly respected and valued his worth. He is now a CEO of an organization, and it is prospering because of his leadership. He has also vowed that he will never treat anyone like he was treated by his former company, and as a result, he enjoys an extremely happy and motivated workforce. If you are to achieve meaningful change, it is important to believe in yourself. Your esteem needs meet your need for recognition, responsibility, achievement, respect, prestige, and self-confidence.

The final level in Maslow's hierarchy is self-actualization. Self-actualization is the stage where you realize the significance you hold and your purpose for being. You realize that you are making the most of your abilities and are making an impact on your environment. It is here that you achieve your potential, a sense of accomplishment, and satisfaction. Your true creative nature is realized at this level. You are in touch with the genuineness of your life, and it holds deep and meaningful purpose for you. You are constantly striving to be the best person you can be and to reach your full potential as a human being. Maslow best described self-actualization as:

"An episode or spurt in which the episodes of the person come together in a particularly and intensely enjoyable way, and in which he is more integrated and less split, more open for experience, more idiosyncratic, more perfectly expressive or spontaneous, or fully functioning, more creative, more humorous, more ego-transcending, more independent of his own needs, etc. He becomes in these episodes more truly himself, more perfectly actualizing his potentialities, closer to the core of his being, more fully human. Not only are these his happiest and most thrilling moments, but they are also moments of greatest maturity, individualization, fulfillment—in a word, his healthiest moments."

It is important to realize that you cannot fulfill all of your own needs. You can meet many of them; however, in many cases it will be necessary to go outside of yourself to have these needs met. Throughout my early life, I was dependent on my parents to meet my physiological and safety needs. I have been, and continue to be, dependent on my wife, my family-friends, and co-workers for my socialization needs. Teachers, mentors, family, and friends have been responsible for many of my esteem needs. The combination of all of these needs being met and my continuing growth, maturity, and development has led to the fulfillment of many of my self-actualization needs.

In making meaningful change, it is important to realize how the ebb and flow of your needs as well as how they are, or are not, met can have a large effect on how successful you are in reaching your desired goals.

When you face a new situation, there is bound to be information that you need to find out if you are going to function properly under those circumstances. It will inevitably be necessary for you to gather and learn new information that will be essential to successful transition to your desired state. Using the information is not always that difficult, but finding it is usually the toughest part.

Finding information, or conducting research, is considered by many to be a long and tedious process. This is generally because the unknown presents a formidable obstacle in getting them where they want to be. Many businesses, for example, need to conduct research, or get information, about their customers, their marketplace, or their competition for them to be successful in developing business strategies. If they skip this part of the process, the result is often a business action plan that does not work because it was based on incorrect information.

Webster's defines research as a "careful or diligent search; studious and critical inquiry and examination aimed at the discovery and interpretation of new knowledge." When you are looking for facts or information that is important to you in the change process, all you are really doing is examining the facts around you in an effort to discover or find some new interpretation of knowledge.

You would probably be amazed at how much information is readily available. All you really have to do is play private investigator and go looking for it. I wrote an earlier version of this piece about twenty years ago. At that time, I would spend hours in the library working with these wonderful people called librarians, who would help me locate all kinds of reference books and resources where I could find the information that I needed to review to help formulate my thoughts. Today, I am sitting in my office working on my computer. I have music playing through the iTunes library; I can see if an e-mail comes in while I am working; and I am typing this book through my word processing program. If I come to a part where I would like a little more information on a subject, I can switch over to the Internet, where I can use any number of search engines to look up and get access to thousands of databases holding information that I need. If I get stuck and need some help, I can e-mail or call any number of libraries to ask for assistance. Technology has made the search process so much easier, and there is virtually no reason why you cannot get access to any of the information you need.

You would also be amazed at how much information your friends or acquaintances have access to. Information can come from the most unlikely sources, but you must be willing to ask for it. Here is a good rule of thumb: When you are looking for some specific information that you cannot find, ask anyone and everyone. You will be amazed at what information or leads you can obtain this way. I don't know about you, but I am my favorite subject. Like most people, if you ask me about me, I will probably tell you more than you want to know. People are generally flattered when you ask them about themselves, their ideas and opinions, and their professions or jobs. You will be surprised at how helpful people will be when you ask them about an area where they have a great deal of expertise. The idiom "flattery will get you everywhere" is true.

I was once working with a friend of mine who had lost his job and decided that he wanted to make a career shift. He was always intrigued by, and wanted to work in, the field of development, specifically at the college or university level; however, his experience to date had been in sales. He really did not know the first thing about development and did not know how to find out more. I kept suggesting that he make a list of all of the people or organizations he knew in the development field and start asking for informational interviews. An informational interview is where you meet someone with no other expressed purpose than to gain new information about the field, industry, or company that person is employed in. After resisting for about six months and complaining constantly about his lack of progress, he decided to act on my suggestion. He was amazed how much he learned about development. Within three months, he had contacted the development department at every major college and university in the area. He had also developed an extensive network of contacts within the industry and was quite well versed in the field. More importantly, he received two job offers and is now working in the field. The two principles he kept in mind throughout the process were:

- **Always make sure you have another interview to go to; and**

- **Always get at least one new contact name from each interview.**

One of the most important resources you will need in this process is a strong support network. I cannot begin to tell you how many people have been there to help me in my life. Support can be essential when going through a challenging time. You may need advice or direction. You may need reassurance or guidance on how to handle situations. You may just need a friendly ear to listen to your fears and frustration or a reassuring voice to tell you that you can get through this and that everything will work out. This support can come from any number of sources—from a spouse or significant other, a family member or friend, or perhaps a mentor or professional colleague. It could be a professional association or other support group. It could be a book, a movie, or other inspirational message. Don't underestimate the importance and value of support in this effort.

There are any number of resources that you can consult to better understand yourself or your situation, and many sources you can rely on for the information you need to make a successful change. All you need to do is seek them out and utilize them.

CHAPTER SEVEN

THE PLAN

"A goal without a plan is just a wish."

ANTOINE DE SAINT-EXUPERY

I think that a dream in and of itself is just a series of random thoughts that have no connection with reality. I think that if you are to make the transition from a dream state to reality, you need to associate some definite concrete thoughts on how you are going to do it.

I have often dreamed about things I would like to happen. I have imagined conversations I would have with people who upset me. I composed letters to the editor in my head countless times to express my opinion on various issues. If I focus on only the finished piece, it seems like such a huge feat to make the picture in my head become real. When I start to fantasize about how I can work on making this picture a reality, however, the project becomes much more realistic and achievable.

One of the first homes I bought had an unfinished basement. This was where I stored my exercise equipment, and I spent many hours in that basement working out. For the longest time, I wanted to finish off that basement. I don't know how many times I was down in that large, open, empty space thinking about how nice the room would be and how much bigger my house would be if that basement were a completed living space. It wasn't until I started to imagine myself doing the work and how I would accomplish it that the thought became reality. I began standing in that room imagining where I would place the frame, how I would secure it, and how much wood I would need to complete the job. Next, I thought about the electrical wiring and the Sheetrock to cover up the frame. Then I thought about the ceiling and whether it would be a drop ceiling or Sheetrocked and how I could get that up by myself. Then I thought about painting, carpeting, and decorating. It was not long after I started doing this that I actually began the work, and after completing the project, I was amazed at how well the finished project matched my dreams of how it would enlarge my home.

Visualization is an important part of the change process. A contractor would not think about building a house before a blueprint was drawn up. Think about that for a moment. What is a blueprint anyway? Isn't it merely the architect's visualization of what the house should look like, where everything will go, and how much material will be needed to complete the job? Before that house can be build, someone must take the time to develop a mental image of what the structure will look like and record it on paper. If you are taking a trip in your car, don't you need to consult a map or make sure the car has a navigation system to make sure you can get to your destination the quickest and easiest way possible? If you are planning a party, don't you need to make a list of where it will be held, who you are going to invite, what refreshments and food you are going to provide, what the themes and activities will be, and what supplies or arrangements will need to be made before the party? Top athletes often talk about how they visualize their actions on the field long before they ever take place. A batter visualizes contacting the ball; a quarterback visualizes releasing the ball in a perfect spiral; a winger visualizes shooting the puck in the top corner of the net; and a swimmer visualizes a perfect entry into the water with a minimum of splash. Aren't these merely forms of visualization translated into actionable items?

The hardest part of any action is the decision to act. Once you begin, you are often astounded at how easy the action itself was, but you can become immobilized trying to get off the dime and begin. Nowhere is this truer than in trying to make changes in your life. You procrastinate and find excuses, asking yourself what if. You can come up with a reason for doing everything except what you really need to do. I have mentioned that I am a runner and that winter is the toughest time of the year for me to be dedicated to my sport. It is often very tough to get out the door when it is below freezing. Many times I have found myself rationalizing that it is too early to go outside, that I should wait until it warms up in the afternoon, or that I will just read the newspaper or have a quick cup of coffee before I go. The best rationalization of all is that I ran yesterday, so I really don't have to run today. Before I know it, it's too late to get my run in, and I have forfeited an activity that is important to me and is a critical part of my plan to get and stay healthy. When I procrastinate, I am the big loser.

In large part, the reason you delay making changes is that you are afraid of the outcome. So many of us so desperately want to control the outcome of our actions that we are willing to wait until the opportunity is just right or until we have the sense that it will work out just the way we want it to. The result is that we often wait too long, or in many cases, never do anything at all, and thus remain where we are—stuck!

The focus of this chapter is on visualizing what the change you want to make will look like, how it can manifest itself, and then making the decision to act. It asks you to believe in the process of change and to trust that if you take some responsibility for undertaking the action, the outcome will be OK. It is hard to trust in something you are not sure you believe in. It forces you to look at your faith and belief system. This is an even tougher decision to make if you are a person who wants control. It also asks you to accept the outcome as good and right for you at this time. This is difficult for anyone to swallow, especially if it is a concept that you have never practiced before. It taxes the full scope and limits of your faith, but it is a necessary step if you are to realize change in your life. The reality is that sooner or later you will need to change your current situation, so the sooner you do it, the sooner you will realize the benefit of the change.

If you choose to look at this process in a positive light, it frees you from a lot of pressure. If you only take responsibility for the effort and accept that the outcome is out of your control, you don't need to spend a lot of time and energy worrying about the result of your actions. This does not mean you will not need to take responsibility for the consequences of your actions, just that the consequences are really out of your control. You can find release and freedom in channeling all of your energy into taking the necessary steps for effective change instead of trying to control the situation. If you have made a commitment to yourself or organization, have faith that you are not alone in this effort, and that if and when you need help, it will present itself, this step in the process becomes easier to put into practice.

The following questions will help you focus on some steps you can take to make change achievable in your life:

- Why do you want to make this change? What do you hope to realize as a result of the changes you want to undertake? How will this make your life or organization different and/or better?

  _____

  _____

- Where do you want this change to take place? Is there a specific area of your life and/or organization? Is there a specific place or geographic location involved?

  _____

  _____

- When do you want this change to occur? Is there a specific timeline or deadline that you have in mind or need to adhere to? When do you anticipate achieving these objectives and goals?

  _____

  _____

- How will you make all of this happen? What actions must take place for this vision to be realized? What steps can you take to make these changes happen? What actions are out of your hands?

  _____

  _____

- Who is involved in this change besides you? Who else besides you will be affected by the consequences of your change? How will they be affected and how will they react to and/or participate in the process of change? What is their attitude toward these changes?

_____

_____

The great philosopher Yogi Berra is reported to have said, "If you don't know where you're going, you might end up somewhere else!" How many times have you found yourself lost because you did not know where you were going? You were walking around aimlessly not knowing if you were coming or going, simply because you lacked direction. It is critical to have a mission or purpose in your life or in the life of your organization. If you do not, you will be like the proverbial rudderless ship going around in circles because it has no way to steer.

The passage of time has been marked by the history of men and women who have embarked on a mission of one sort or another. Columbus's mission was to find a shorter path to the Orient. Along the way, he discovered that the world was not really flat and that there was a wondrous new place, which became the Americas. The balance of power in Europe continually shifted from the nineth century to the fifteenth century because Europe and the Church of Rome were on a mission to make the world a haven for Christianity. You still see consequences of the mission of the Crusades in the actions of terrorists that went well into the twenty-first century. Alexander Graham Bell fought off failure after failure in his mission to help the deaf because he believed he could project a human voice over long distances through the marvels of modern science. Amelia Earhart went down in history because of her mission to be the first woman to fly an airplane around the world.

Right or wrong, these people were driven by their desire to achieve their ultimate purpose. So it must be with us. If you want to realize change in your life or organization, you must set your sights on an ultimate end and dedicate yourself to achieving it. You must give your life some meaning, to achieve some purpose, to self-actualize. It is that purpose that will provide the motivation to face and overcome the obstacles that are inevitable along the way.

A mission does not need to be a lofty or grandiose thing. It can be very simple. Somewhere along the way, I realized that my mission was to leave the world a little better for my having been in it. I did not have to save it from nuclear destruction, or discover a cure for cancer, or even donate a small fortune to the poor. For me it came down to the fact that if I used my talents to help someone and to make them feel a little better for the experience of having met me, then I had accomplished my mission. It could simply be saying a kind word, doing someone a favor, doing work that made a positive contribution to society or to the community, or it could even be writing a book like this one that would produce good. My mission gave me a lot of latitude, but it also gave me a lot of direction.

If you want to focus and direct your personal or organizational life, it is important to clearly identify your mission. A mission simply identifies who you are, what you want to do or be, what you stand for, what you want to offer that others need, what skills or talents you possess, what you want to be remembered for, how you want others to perceive you, and what your philosophy of living is all about. Noted management consultant Peter Drucker (1977) said, "Only a clear definition of the mission and purpose of the business makes possible clear and realistic business objectives. It is the foundation for priorities, strategies, plans and work assignments." The same is true for life in general. How can you plan for your life if you do not know what you want it to stand for and how you want to live it? How can you direct an organization if you don't know what that organization is all about and why it exists? I think many people go through a so-called midlife crisis simply because they wake up one day and realize that they have been breezing through life without really knowing where they were going and why.

Vision and visualization ask you to look at what you see happening in your life or organization. Your mission states your commitment to making that vision a reality. It can be a reminder of what you want to achieve, what you want to stand for, or what you want to be remembered for when people think about you. A mission can keep you focused, on track, and committed to your vision and goals.

Questions to consider in developing your personal or organizational mission include:

- **What has been your personal or organizational mission to this point?**

  _____

- **What _do_ you stand for personally or as an organization?**

  _____

- **What _should_ you stand for personally or as an organization?**

  _____

  _____

- **What are your basic beliefs or values?**

  _____

  _____

- **What kind of person and/or organization are you?**

  _____

- **What kind of person and/or organization do you want to be?**

  _____

- **What kind of people, companies, organizations, or customers do you interact with?**

  _____

- **What are some of the needs and expectations of these people, organizations, or customers?**

  _____

- What are the ways that you meet these needs and expectations? Do you do a poor, adequate, or exceptional job of meeting those needs and expectations?

  _____

  _____

- How do you want people, organizations, customers, or the public in general to perceive you?

  _____

- Should your mission change in the next five years? If so, how?

  _____

  _____

In an earlier chapter I talked about the importance of goals. We examined Webster's definition of a goal as "the end toward which effort is directed: aim." When formulating your plan, outlining clear goals will help you develop detailed strategies to effectively achieve those goals. Pablo Picasso once said, "Our goals can only be reached through the vehicle of a plan. There is no other route to success."

As you begin to outline your goals for change, it is vital to ensure that they align with your value system. Your values represent your personal sense of right and wrong. They are the principles that you choose to live by. They are the beliefs that enable us to make decisions on particular courses of action throughout our lives. They help us decide exactly what it is we want to do with our lives. They are the moral compass that guides us through the difficult ethical decisions we will have to make as we traverse through our individual journeys. They are in essence the part of your character that defines your existence.

Your values are what define your character. How you act and how you treat other people is usually the standard by which other people measure who you are. It is difficult to form an honest and accurate opinion about someone one way or another until you spend some time with that person and see how they behave in their day-to-day life.

You need to see how they operate, how they interact with others, how they are affected by different situations, how they react to challenges and opportunities, how they think, what they say, what is important to them, and what is not. Generally, you need to see how they live their lives. I remember reading an article about a corporate manager who would never hire a new employee without first taking them out for a meal. He would observe how they treated the wait staff. He knew they would be on their best behavior with him, but he thought the way they reacted to the wait staff would be a good indicator of how they treated people in the normal course of their day-to-day activities.

You generally act according to your value system. If integrity is an important part of your value system, then you likely behave like a person with high integrity. If caring about others is an important value to you, then you probably show a lot of care and concern for other people around you. If loyalty and dependability are important values in your life, then generally you are a person who can be counted on to come through.

Your value system guides your day-to-day activities and decisions and shapes how you interact with other people. For example, if honesty is a very important value to you, it would be stressful and difficult for you to spend a day telling someone untruths. Assume that someone gave you a piece of business information and told you not to disclose that information to anyone. Then for the balance of the day, business associates called you with specific, direct questions requesting the information you had on this very subject. How difficult do you think it would be to successfully carry on these conversations if one of your values was to be completely honest with people at all times?

Your core values come to you from all different sources. The primary source is your family system dictated by your parents and other close family members. Your value system is developed very early in life, so you generally adopt the same values as your family. As you grow, your friends are a source of values as well. When you were younger, how many times did you behave in a manner that was questionable, justifying your behavior by saying, "My friends say it's OK, so it must be!" Teachers and religious leaders are also a source for developing your values. Many of my political and economic values were formed through the influence of various teachers I met, and those values were continually influenced throughout my education.

Role models and heroes are also a source of value development. Each generation has had their share of heroes who influenced that generation, whether they were real or imaginary characters. Political leaders like Theodore and Franklin Roosevelt, Winston Churchill, Charles de Gaulle, John and Robert Kennedy, and Mikhail Gorbachev greatly influenced the people of their countries. In the US presidential election of 2008, there were three heroic figures battling for the highest office in the land. John McCain was a genuine war hero; Hillary Clinton, who was vying to become the first female president in US history, served as a role model for women throughout the world; and Barack Obama, who stood to be our first African American president, delivered a motivational message to millions of Americans and energized political interest in a way not seen in the country for years. How many young people throughout the decades have been inspired by imaginary heroes like Superman, the Lone Ranger, Red Rider, Barney, Kermit, Big Bird, Elmo, or even real heroes like Mr. Rogers? Sports heroes and music and entertainment celebrities are held in high public scrutiny because of the influence they have over the value systems of younger people. Business mentors, professional people, philosophers, authors, and counselors all have an impact on your values as you go through life attempting to determine what is personally right and wrong for you.

It is important to identify the core values that you live your life by. You need to assess if they are still appropriate not only for who you are, but also for who you want to be. You will also need to determine if these values are realistic and attainable. There are many people who talk a good game about their value system and what they hold as important principles to espouse; however, when it comes down to doing it, their behavior often does not mirror their words. You will need to assess the value system of the culture you operate in as well, be it your family, social, community, or work environment, to determine if it measures up to your values and vice versa.

Very often people think that they can live by two different sets of values. I have met people who believe, and have seen behavior to confirm that belief, that in different situations it is appropriate and ethical to operate under two distinct value systems. They believe that it is OK to be slightly dishonest and ruthless in business for example because everyone else is, and "it's just business." In their personal lives, however, they believe they are completely honest and trustworthy. I personally find this type of belief to be highly contradictory and very confusing. I am always, or at least try to be, the same person in every situation I am involved in. I may be more formal in one or more relaxed in another, I may dress differently from one scenario to another, or the subject matter or occasion may be different, but my intellectual process and value system are always identical. If I try to tell myself I can switch values to meet the occasion, I am only deluding myself. It is my experience that people who try to operate under two or more different sets of values only wind up experiencing a lot of trouble, not to mention serious credibility gaps.

In his book *Good to Great*, Jim Collins (2001) talks about two key unique traits that he found in the leaders of the eleven "great" companies he studied; they are intense professional will and extreme personal humility. Collins defines professional will as "an unwavering resolve to do whatever must be done to produce the best long-term results, no matter how difficult." Of humility he says a great leader "demonstrates a compelling modesty . . .; acts with quiet, calm determination . . .; channels ambition into the company, not the self . . .; looks out the window, not in the mirror, to apportion credit for the success of the company . . ." These are character traits you must bring to the change process if you are to be successful. You must be willing to rise above any challenge or adversity and maintain your focus on achieving your final goal, doing whatever it takes to fulfill your mission. It is also critical to remain humble, as change is rarely realized alone. As I once heard Robert Schuler say, "Humility is realizing that you need help and being able to ask for it."

Marcus and Smith in *Egonomics* (2007) took Collin's key leadership attributes a little further. They identify three key traits of effective leaders: humility, curiosity, and veracity. Their definition of humility mirrors that of Collins. They say curiosity "drives exploration of ideas. Curiosity gives us permission and courage to test what we think, feel, and believe to be true, reminding us we don't know everything about anything." According to Marcus and Smith, "Veracity is the habitual pursuit of and adherence to truth. It helps make the undiscussables discussable and closes the gap between what we think is going on and what's really going on." As you embark on the change process, you need to be ever curious, looking for information and answers to questions that can lead you forward on the path you desire. Veracity will keep you from the temptation to accept false or misleading information or beliefs generated either internally or externally as you evaluate your current and desired states. The old saying is true; the truth will set you free! In the quest for change, it is highly likely that your personal will helps you constantly keep moving forward, while humility keeps you grounded in reality. Curiosity will keep you questioning and analyzing the consequences and results of your actions, while veracity will keep you always seeking the truth in what you see and find around you.

You may also find yourself in situations where you believe you must go against your value system to be successful. I remember specific times when I was starting my own business when I made business decisions that went against my value system. I believed at the time that I needed to make these decisions to be successful. I subsequently learned that they were not good business decisions and that they were not necessary to the survival of my business. As a matter of fact, in most of these situations I would have made better and more profitable decisions if I had stuck to my values.

You may also find that as you grow and change the values you did not consider important then are now very much so. A big part of the change process is facing new experiences and situations. Quite often your old values do not work, and you need to rethink or abandon them and find those values within you that will work to help you maintain your integrity and self-esteem. In making successful change it is important to be true to your value system and to ensure that the circumstances of the change you are about to make will not compromise those values at all.

No change can happen in your life or organization without a plan. If you decide to take a vacation and drive to Florida, would you just jump in your car and start driving? Probably not. You would have to take into consideration how you would get there, what roads you would take, how many days it would take to get there, how much it would cost in gas and tolls, if you would need to stop overnight and where. And that's just getting there. You would need to decide where you would stay, what clothes you would take, what you would do while you were there, how much money you would need for food and entertainment. In short, you would need to think through each phase so you would be prepared before and during your trip. You would need to plan out your vacation.

Change is a lot like taking a trip. It does not happen automatically or magically, and it requires some effort on your part. It requires you to think about the change you want to make and what steps can best help you to make that change. If you blindly rush off on this adventure, chances are you will forget a vital step and get detoured or have to return to your starting point and begin again.

Have you ever purchased a Christmas gift that required some assembly? If you answered yes, then you might have experienced the frustration of sitting up on Christmas Eve trying to assemble this gift you purchased for someone, most likely a child, before they wake up on Christmas morning. I know when I am in a situation like this, I tend to grab my tools and get right at assembly. Usually, I get midway through the project and either have one piece too many or something is not quite working right. In most cases, it traces back to the fact that I did not take time to think about how I was going to approach the project, or simply did not read the directions. It usually takes me about twice as long to get the present assembled than if I had thought about what I was about to do, or at least tried to figure out the directions.

I have worked with hundreds of small business owners over the course of my career, and I am amazed at how many of them jumped right into their businesses without taking the time to develop a plan and identify the steps necessary to be successful. And with many of them, if they do take the time to develop a plan, either put it up on the shelf or do something reactionary the first time they run into a problem. They put a lot of thought into developing a strategic plan that lays out the exact steps they need to take to reach their goal; then something comes up to distract and frighten them, and they walk away from their plan, usually before it has had adequate time to work. When you purchase a box of cake mix at the supermarket, the box tells you exactly how you are to prepare that cake in the proper sequence to get the outcome you see pictured on the front of the package. Even the most experienced home baker knows it is important to follow the steps or the result may be less than acceptable. So it must be with the process of change. You need to determine the correct steps to get to your desired goals and give them a chance to work.

In their book *Influencer: The Power to Change Anything*, Kerry Patterson, Joseph Grenny, David Maxfield, Ron McMillan, and Al Switzler (2007) state: "Before people will change their behavior, they have to want to do so, and this means they will have to think differently." Their position is that the most effective way to change is to change negative behavior into positive behavior. In their book, they cite two case studies where life-threatening situations were changed for the better by simply analyzing the circumstances and focusing on three to four negative behaviors that, if altered, could bring about significant change. A simple example of this would be the slightly overweight person who wants to lose the extra bulge that continues to linger around their waistline. This person exercises every day, eats three sensible meals, and has a huge bowl of ice cream with chocolate sauce every evening right before bed. The negative behaviors could be viewed as 1) eating the ice cream, 2) including chocolate sauce, and 3) eating right before bed. If this person eliminated all three negative behaviors, they would probably lose the extra weight in no time at all. Even if they just eliminated the chocolate sauce, they would probably see some result. Or if they ate the ice cream three hours before going to bed, the result would probably be an improvement. In any event, negative behavior replaced by a positive behavior will result in some change.

Change also requires you to be willing to do whatever it takes to get you to your desired goals. This means eliminating those barriers that have stood in your way throughout your personal or organizational life. This is the difficult part. Very often you put limitations on how far you are willing to go or how much risk you are willing to take in making changes. It is critical that you develop the willingness to take the risks and go to any lengths to reach your desired goals.

Developing that willingness to do whatever it takes is very tough. When I am dissatisfied with a certain aspect of my life, it's very easy for me to be ready for a change. As a matter of fact, I usually spend a great deal of time telling just about anyone who will listen just how tired I am of being in a certain place and how I cannot wait for the change to happen. Then they ask what I am doing about it, and I break out in a cold sweat of embarrassment. I am generally more willing to talk about something than I am to take the risk of doing something different.

This step requires that you are willing to go to any lengths to do things differently than you have before to affect a change in your personal or organizational life. If I find myself out of shape and I want to get back to my lean and mean years, I might consider the services of a personal trainer. It would be silly to put off hiring the trainer until my body is in good enough shape where I am not embarrassed to go to the gym. Or, if I know I need to cut back on my food consumption because I have been on the road too long and have been suffering from poor eating habits, so I decide to go on a strict regimen to get my eating back to where it needs to be—except for my nightly bowl of ice cream. I have to ask myself if I am willing to do whatever it takes. Unfortunately, when I reach that point, I have my back against a wall and have no other place to go. If I am to make this change meaningful, I must be willing to take any action no matter what the personal risk or discomfort. Usually after I have taken that risk, I realize just how effortless it really was.

I will always remember watching a televised cartoon version of J.R.R. Tolkien's *The Hobbit* (1937) and a great message it gave me one night. In one scene the principal character Bilbo Baggins stood before a door that would lead him into the lair of the evil dragon Smaug. He paused and turned to the audience and said something to the effect of "The next seven steps are the most difficult I will ever take. It's of little consequence what happens when I pass through that door, that's beyond my control. The difficult part is getting to the door, opening and passing through it." Isn't it true that many of us let our fear of opening the door stop us from realizing what is on the other side? If you are to successfully experience any meaningful change, it is critical that you face your fear and open those doors. You must be willing to face whatever lies on the other side.

What lengths are you willing to go to for personal or organizational change?

For me the hardest part of anything is getting started. Once I get going it is not so bad, but it seems that I resist change until I can resist no longer. There is however something about knowing this that works in my favor. I know that I am going to resist change until I make a commitment to the change. Because I understand how important the commitment is, I know that once I am committed there is absolutely no way that I won't follow through. This is because my ego won't let me admit that I can't accomplish a goal once I have committed to that action or behavior, especially if it is said out loud to another person. So, the key to change for me is to get myself to make the commitment.

Some people can motivate themselves simply by making a commitment to themselves. If you are strong willed and have a strong ego, you can certainly make that commitment. If you feel strong enough about yourself or your ideas that you can stick with a course of action, you may be resolved enough to follow through. After all, you are the one who is ultimately accountable for the commitment. You are also the primary beneficiary of the change.

Generally, I think that in making a commitment it is valuable to involve some other party who can hold you accountable. There is something binding about making this commitment to another, be it your spouse, family, friend, employer, or co-worker. When you commit to another, you put yourself out there, and there is a feeling that you have let the other party down if you do not follow through. It may also help to put your commitment in writing in the form of a contract. Knowing that you are accountable and expected to perform can provide the motivation to follow through on your commitment.

Some people feel more comfortable making a commitment to a spiritual concept of belief. I don't know how many times as a child I bargained with my concept of God for a change that I wanted to make. Many times, it was in the form of a bargain that if God would help me through a particular situation, I would make a commitment to change a particular behavior. I don't know how many times I bargained that if I could pass a test in school I would study hard for the rest of my life. Depending on the strength of their conviction and faith, a commitment to a spiritual entity can often keep people on track and committed to their goals.

Ego also plays a part in making a commitment. I know I do not want to be known as someone who does not follow through on their promises or commitments. I do not want to be seen as a quitter who is not able to complete a project they have started. When I fail to follow through on a commitment, my esteem also suffers. Knowing this helps fuel my desire to successfully complete all of those actions, behavior changes, or projects that I begin and commit to.

Indecision is a terrible thing, and often you can pay a hefty price for not making a commitment to act. Imagine a person standing by the side of a cold swimming pool on a hot summer day. That person can stand there indecisive about whether or not to jump in for a long time. Perhaps they are not sure if they want to get wet, or maybe the water is too cold. Perhaps they will mess up their hair, or any other number of excuses for not taking the plunge. In the meantime, they are standing in the sun sweating and awfully hot. Finally, they decide to jump in and cool off. Once they do, the difficult part is over. They happily swim around trying to determine why they ever had any doubts at all. I find that many people find themselves in this same type of situation. They come to the brink of a decision to take some action to change their current circumstances. They know they want to change; however, they are afraid or unsure or not quite ready to do what it takes to begin the action, so they sit immobilized debating the issue. Once they finally make the commitment to act, they are amazed at how swiftly and easily the process begins. One of the hardest parts of any change is making the commitment to do it.

It seems that once the commitment is made the rest is easy, but it seems to be so hard to make that decision to act. I can want to do something so badly, but it takes me forever to get going because of an old nemesis. That nemesis is one of the vilest and most devastating four-letter *f* words—*fear*. Fear can be a crippler in the process of change. It can be fear of getting hurt, fear of failure, fear of success, or even fear that you don't deserve to be happy. Fear is insidious and it often stops people dead in their tracks. When you are immobilized by fear, it is difficult to see the positive side of anything, and you often get despondent. One of the best ways to dispel fear is to face it head on and do whatever it is that scares you. It also helps to talk about your fear. The feedback from others can often help calm and even conquer your fears, giving you the strength and confidence to go forward. When I began my doctoral program, I was terrified at the thought of writing a dissertation, and I was concerned that I would not be able to get through the program. I did not consider myself to be a scholar, and I was fearful that I would not be able to write in a scholarly fashion that was up to the standards of the university. I had a meeting with my advisor, a brilliant man who earned his PhD at Harvard, to discuss my fears. I had immense respect for this professor for his intelligence, his ability to communicate, and his ability to present and teach new concepts that I had not contemplated in the past. I considered him to be very scholarly, especially since he had received his degree from the prestigious Harvard University. His advice to me made all the difference to my performance in my program. He told me not to worry about my writing and to write in my own voice because that would be the most important and authentic voice I could present. I was very humbled and honored when in my dissertation defense he commented on how scholarly my work had been. The fear that keeps you from realizing your dreams is the worst fear of all.

No matter how, where, or to whom you commit, it is critical that you commit to this process. Without commitment there is seldom conviction; without conviction there is seldom follow through.

John Donne wrote, "No man is an island entire of itself." How right he was; however, how often we try to prove him wrong. I don't know what it is about human beings, but it seems that we are always trying to do everything by ourselves. Have you ever been in a position where you were facing an obstacle that just scared you to death? And rather than admit that you were afraid, you toughed it out and faced that fear all by yourself, shaking and quivering all the way. The fear probably made it twice as hard and made it take twice as long to accomplish the task. If you had only talked to someone, the process of simply admitting your fear would have greatly diminished it right off the bat. Additionally, you would have gotten some support from that person, and chances are they might have encountered the same kind of fear or a similar situation in the past and would have shared their experience with you. Unfortunately, you don't often think about this when you are in the thick of it.

Throughout my career, I traveled a lot for work; on many occasions my wife told me that she thought I liked being away from her. When I was on the road working, I often had a full day. By the time I got back to my hotel room I was ready for bed, and I generally had no problem getting right to sleep. In fact, I was usually so busy that I didn't think much of the fact that I was alone because I had heavy contact with people during the day and was ready for some alone time. Then my wife started a job that required her to do some travel. I found that when I was home alone and went to bed, I had an uneasy feeling because she was not there with me. I was so used to her physical presence at home that I got a little spooked when she was not around.

It is a fact of life that you need the companionship of other people to complete your life. If you did not have others, you would not be able to exist in your own little world, or as Donne said, on your own little island completely devoid of contact or dependence on someone else. You depend on your parents for your very existence and your livelihood and nurturing during the first few years of your life. Then you need other people like family, teachers, and playmates who all play important roles in your development. As you grow, you find mentors and role models who help you shape your life and develop your goals. You are dependent on farmers for food and manufacturers for clothing and other products important for day-to-day life. You need the carpenter to build your homes, transportation workers to help you move from place to place, factory workers for the everyday goods you take for granted, the media for your news and weather. You need utility workers for the water, gas, and electricity you consume every day. You need police and firefighters to protect you. In essence, without other people, your life as you have come to know it would not exist.

Within your work environment you also need people for the organization to function. You need workers to produce your products and services; you need accountants to keep your books; you need people to process orders, answer phones, sell to your customers, etc. You even need someone to issue you a paycheck so you can pay your bills. Without people, organizations would cease to exist.

So why is it you tell yourself that you don't need anyone? Society has created classic messages telling you that you should be tough, independent, and self-sufficient. How many times have you seen the western hero single-handedly facing the outlaw gang, the war hero sneaking into the enemy camp to rescue his comrades, or the frontier woman braving the elements and delivering her child alone while her husband is out looking for food? These are all Hollywood stereotypes. The smart western hero would get a posse, the war hero would only attack in battalion strength, and the frontier woman would not attempt to deliver her baby without a doctor or midwife. The fact is that if humans were meant to be self-sufficient, we would have developed the physical, mental, and emotional capabilities to exist by ourselves. The mere fact that man cannot reproduce by himself suggests that we were not meant to exist alone. No animal on the planet lives on its own in its own habitat. We need the assistance of others to function properly in this life.

I ran a marathon a few years ago that taught me a valuable lesson in realizing the importance of other people. I had run quite a few marathons by this time, and it had been my experience that the last few miles often were quite difficult and sometimes painful. I have always trained hard, but when you are running twenty-six miles there usually comes a point, especially when you are running alone, when you start to tell yourself that you cannot possibly run one more step, and you may struggle to finish the race. This marathon was completely different. I never once struggled. In fact, when I finished the race, I felt like I could go on for another five miles. It was a glorious run, and I had fun the whole way. The thing that was different from other races was that I did not run alone. I started out with a group of five friends. One friend, who knew she might have a difficult race, asked if she could run with me and if would I help her get through the race. We ran stride for stride for 26.2 miles, and by focusing on her race and how she was doing, I was able to forget about myself. As a result, I had the run of my life. Not only did she finish, but she finished thirty-five minutes faster than her previous best marathon time. I experienced what management consultants have been talking about for years when they say that teamwork can increase the effectiveness and efficiency of any work previously done by individuals alone.

You depend on other people, and they are essential in your life. In many cases you do not even know or have contact with all the people who influence your daily life. In other cases, these people are well known to you. In those areas that are most important to you, especially in the process of change, you can have a say in who will give you the assistance you need. Quite often you are required to go outside of yourself and solicit specific help. Unfortunately, just as often your ego tells you that you really should be able to do all these things by yourself. It is essential to get past your ego, identify how, why, and from whom you need help, and then go out and ask for it. You may have heard the expression "stick with the winners." This is an appropriate slogan to keep in mind when seeking assistance. If you seek advice and assistance from people who have success in the areas where you want to make changes, you are more likely to get the kind of results you desire.

Part of the process involves communication. Simply talking to people about your situation and what you are attempting to accomplish through the change process can start to bring you the answers you need to complete it. When you are out in the world talking about yourself and the changes you desire, things begin to happen. The process of acting puts an energy flow in motion that helps us to be in the position to meet and communicate with individuals who can do us the most good. Merely sitting at home and hoping that change will take place by osmosis will do us absolutely no good. It is in talking to people about your situation that you begin to realize the answers to your questions. When you begin to talk, assistance begins to flow to you, but you must be willing to take the risk to open up and communicate about yourself and your situation.

Sometimes the help can come from the most unexpected places. Early on in my career I accepted a job in a field that was not quite what I thought it would be. I knew that if I wanted to continue in this field, I would need to get a specialized degree in an area that I was not really interested in. I knew I wanted to go back into advertising and communications, a field I had worked in before accepting this job; however, I was lost on how to go about doing it. I made a lunch appointment with a friend with the express purpose of asking him how I should go about looking for a job. As we were walking from his office to the restaurant, my friend waived to an acquaintance he saw on the street. After we had passed his friend, he told me I should go have a talk with this gentleman as he was an important executive with the largest advertising agency in town. When we got back to his office after lunch, he called his acquaintance and arranged an interview for me. I subsequently met with the gentleman, and he connected me with some people within the firm who were looking for someone with just the experience I possessed. I was ultimately offered the position and worked for the firm for a number of years, in what proved to be one of the most important development periods in my career. If I had not been willing to talk to my friend about my fear and confusion about making a career move, I might not have found that job opportunity, which proved to be so important to my career growth.

If you are going to escape from the isolation of your present situation and make effective change in your personal or organizational life, you are going to need some help. You have already started that process by reading this book, but reading alone is not going to cut it. You need the interaction, the experience, and the energy generated by connecting with another human being. You must locate at least one person, and hopefully more, who can assist you in this process.

Help can come in many ways from many different people. It can come from people within your organization, a mentor or advisor, a co-worker, a family member, a casual acquaintance, or even a perfect stranger. A big part of the process is to look around and to take stock of all the resources at your disposal. You will probably be shocked at just how many there are.

Think about the resources available to you right now. Ask yourself the following questions:

- In what specific areas will you require assistance? Who do you know that can directly or indirectly help you in this area or refer you to the appropriate party?

  _____

  _____

- Will you need assistance with professional support? Emotional support? Financial support? Professional development? Counseling? Education? Skills training?

  _____

  _____

- Who do you need to support you, and what kind of support do you need in this effort?

  _____

  _____

- What other actions can you take or what activities can you undertake to get you out of isolation and potentially provide aid or resources for you in this process?

  _____

  _____

Empowerment can be an overused word. Businesses talk about empowering their people so they can be more effective, and the firm can be more efficient. Self-help literature talks about personal empowerment as a means of achieving personal goals. Many people however don't have the foggiest idea what empowerment means.

According to the dictionary, the word empower means to authorize. Therefore, if a business empowers its employees to work more effectively, it gives them the authority necessary to make decisions and take action that will make them more effective workers. If you are talking about personal empowerment, that means you are giving yourself the authority to take appropriate action to reach your goals.

You may be asking, "Don't I automatically empower myself?" The answer in many cases is no. You often set up barriers and give yourself messages that keep you from taking the steps necessary to realize the goals you want to achieve. I don't know how many times in my life when I was dieting in an attempt to lose weight that I told myself, *Oh, don't even bother trying. You will never lose that weight.* Then, of course, I would determine that it was indeed hopeless and continue the eating behavior that got me in trouble to begin with. The negative messages reinforced the negative behavior, and in effect allowed me to stay where I was, in that comfortable familiar place. It wasn't until I began to change the negative messages and empower myself to live a lifestyle that included healthy eating and exercise habits that I was able to get the weight off for good.

After years of constant travel, some bad habits got me in a place physically that I did not like. After some feeble attempts on my own and with some support and motivation from my wife, I hired a personal trainer to help me develop an exercise program that would get me back where I wanted to be. I met with him weekly, and he empowered me to look at exercise in a different way than I had in the past. He challenged me weekly to do activities and exercises that I had never done before, and that by my own reckoning, I would not have believed I could do. As a result of his direct and indirect empowerment, I made physical changes that were far superior to what I had hoped for.

I frequently find that self-esteem is the catalyst or the detriment to self-empowerment. When I am feeling good about myself, or my organization for that matter, I can accomplish objectives that I once thought were unattainable. The flip side of the coin, unfortunately, is that when I am feeling bad about myself there seems to be absolutely nothing I can do about my situation. Your attitude about yourself and your situation is so critical, yet ironically, it is about the only thing you can control. I have been in situations where the smallest annoyance sets me off on a tirade because I am not feeling good and positive about myself. I have also been in situations where I realize complete serenity in the face of a major crisis, simply because I feel pretty good about myself and know that I can weather any storm. I have also been able to turn a negative circumstance into a positive one simply by changing my attitude. The funny thing about attitude is that you get to choose whether to make it positive or negative.

There are many things you can do to empower yourself to make the changes that you want to realize in your personal or organizational life. You can simply give yourself permission to make change. A good part of my early life was spent trying to live up to the expectations of my parents, mentors, spouse, children, friends, clients, co-workers, and students. I was trying to live up to everyone else's expectations, or at least what I thought they expected of me, instead of my own. I ultimately discovered that the first step to changing this was to examine these expectations, determine whose they were, and if I really thought they were valid and important. For example, I grew up with the notion that people expected me to be perfect, which I thought was an unattainable goal. Those old familiar words "that's good, but you can always do better" were constantly ringing in my ears. As a result, I never thought my best efforts were sufficient, so I either placed outrageous performance demands on myself, or I did nothing rather than face the disappointment of being substandard. I had to tell myself that my best was good enough to empower myself to do the best job possible, and to feel happy and proud of my effort. This was not a simple task. It took much effort and repetition of the message for me to get to the point where I automatically and genuinely said that my best was pretty darn good.

Other people are very important in delivering empowerment messages to us. The voices of your parents are the first ones you hear, and what those voices say can make a big difference in how you approach life. The messages you get from your friends, teachers, mentors, employers, friends, and others play a large part in shaping who you are as people and how you choose to live your life. I have received some extremely empowering messages from mentors throughout my career. Two that have served me very well as I matured and grew in my life and career are: "Always remain flexible," and "I don't care how many mistakes you make as long as you don't make the same mistake twice." The first told me to look at all of the options around me; the more open I was to changing my position the better off I would be. The history of my career has been about adapting to the circumstances in which I found myself and choosing to follow the path that most appealed to me. This affirmation has served me well. The second piece of advice gave me the freedom to risk. I knew that it would be OK to try and fail as long as I learned from my experiences and used that knowledge positively the next time I was faced with a similar situation. I have benefited greatly throughout my life from the wisdom, help, and empowerment of others, and I feel that it is my responsibility to pass along my knowledge, experience, support, and empowering messages to others.

You can also use affirmations to help empower yourself to make the changes you desire. Affirmations are uplifting slogans or sayings you can repeat over and over to reinforce positive thoughts. Affirmations can be simple, or they can be complex, but they must be positive. In his book *The Power of Positive Thinking*, Dr. Norman Vincent Peale (1958) speaks of the power of positive thoughts and accompanying messages. Dr. Peale said that his daily regiment was to rise every morning and repeat three times out loud the affirmation: "I can do all things through God who strengthens me." Try repeating this or a similar affirmation out loud, and you will realize how difficult it is to resist the positive thought associated with the words. Develop your own list of positive affirmations that you can use throughout the day, during good moments as well as difficult ones. This will be a positive step that you can take to ensure healthy empowerment.

As you think about how you want to empower or authorize yourself or your organization to make positive change, think about the following questions:

- **What are some of the expectations that you have for yourself? Are they yours or others, and are they expectations you want to live with?**

  _____

  _____

- **What are some of the barriers that get in the way of empowering you, or others?**

  _____

  _____

- **What are some things you can do to overcome these barriers and empower yourself to change these actions or thoughts?**

  _____

  _____

- **What are some of the negative messages you give yourself that keep you stuck in your present behavior or position?**

  _____

  _____

- **How can you reword those messages to change them from negative to positive thoughts?**

  _____

  _____

- What positive affirmations can you or your organization adopt to help empower you to make the changes you desire?

_____

_____

All of life is a risk. You do not know what is going to happen to you from one day to the next—or even one moment to the next. How many times have you heard someone say, "Who knows what will happen? For all I know I could walk out the front door and get run over by a bus." This is such a true statement, but one we all seem to take for granted. Most of us do not consciously think about living or dying. You don't think about what would happen if suddenly the plants stopped producing oxygen, and you could not get enough air to breathe. You unconsciously accept the fact that your ecological system will continue to work, and you will breathe normally from one minute to the next. This is because you have been conditioned through experience to expect that there will normally be an abundant supply of oxygen in your solar system. You become complacent and take many of the normal events of life for granted.

For years, scientists have been warning about the effects of carbon emissions and other pollutants on the ozone layer and the possibility of climate change. Yet we ignore these warnings until catastrophic events like hurricanes, tsunamis, and changing weather patterns hit. We have heard warnings for years about the dangers of our dependence on petroleum-based products. Detroit automakers resisted the call for more fuel efficient and alternative energy cars until gas prices of nearly four dollars per gallon and increasingly more efficient and hybrid competition from foreign manufacturers brought US automotive companies to the brink of bankruptcy. Today, American auto manufacturers are talking about an all-electric lineup of new models by the year 2030. This lack of foresight and unwillingness to take risks to innovate and try new ideas of operating has led to near disastrous consequences on many fronts.

Unfortunately, we are not experienced in all things. New events and situations that we have never experienced often cause fear to arise in us. As we discussed earlier, we suffer from all kinds of fear, from fear of failure to fear of success to fear of not being accepted on ad infinitum. When you have never experienced a situation, you are often afraid to take the risk to try it because you do not know what the outcome will be. Many people, for example, are afraid of the dark. It is not that they are necessarily afraid of the dark as much as they are afraid of what they cannot see. For those afraid of the dark, walking into a dark room naturally should present an obstacle to them, but many of those same people have previously experienced the phenomenon of electricity and the electric light bulb. They know instinctively that when they walk into a dark room and trigger the circuit that routes electricity from its source to the electric light bulb in the room, the space will be illuminated. They don't necessarily think about it in those detailed terms, but they know by experience that if they are scared in the dark and turn on a light, then the dark and their fear will go away. They have probably done it thousands of times, beginning when they were small children lying in their beds afraid of the dark. They were scared, began crying, and mom or dad came in to see what was wrong. The first thing that mom or dad did was turn on the light, and immediately the fear began to fade. They took the risk of calling out, and then mom or dad came and eliminated their fear simply by walking in the room. Unfortunately, overcoming fear is not as simple as turning on a light. But it may help you to remember a circumstance such as that one where you were able to overcome your fear by taking a simple risk.

By definition, risk is exposure to possible danger or loss. It is amazing how far people will go to avoid danger. We all want to feel safe and secure. Many people will stay in an uncomfortable place simply because it is familiar. There is an old fable that Peter Senge (1990) uses in his book *The Fifth Discipline* to describe how people can be deceived when they are trying to make change. The parable of the boiled frog tells of a frog that is placed in a pot of water; as the water is gradually heated up, the frog makes no attempt to escape. As a matter of fact, as the water becomes hotter, the frog becomes more and more complacent, until finally the frog is immobilized and cannot escape the boiling water even if it wanted to. It is more comfortable to stay in a familiar place than to take a risk. Unfortunately, the longer you stay in that comfortable place the harder it is to leave. Quite often people find themselves boiled alive by a situation that would have been very easy to change.

Fear of loss is another reason why people will expend more effort to protect what they have than they will to obtain something better. The old saying "a bird in the hand is better than two in the bush" applies here. A risk is not a guarantee of anything, and many people want guarantees. Their philosophy is that it is better to stay with what they have rather than to risk losing it and getting nothing in return. Even if the gain is far superior to what they already have, the threat of loss is so strong for some people that they will stay in mediocrity rather than take the risk to be successful.

It is important to remember that failure is part of the learning process. You learn from your mistakes; part of learning is correcting the errors in your actions. How many of you started walking when you were a newborn? You could barely hold up your head. It was not until your body and your bones got stronger that you were able to hold up your head, then sit up, then crawl, and then with much effort, walk. You probably fell on your backside more than once. You needed to learn about balance and how to put one foot in front of the other in a way that would help you get from one place to another, usually at a hectic pace because you were afraid you would land back on your rump. You had the tenacity to keep on taking that risk and trying to walk. This is the kind of spirit you need to bring to the change process.

You always hear stories of all the great heroes of history and captains of industry who found fame and fortune by building successful organizations. How often, however, do you hear about their failures? Abraham Lincoln lost numerous elections before he was elected president. Harry Truman had a haberdashery business that went bankrupt. Thomas Edison had thousands of patents that produced no tangible products. Most successful people have had numerous setbacks and failures, but they were always willing to take the risk to try again and persevere until they found success. So it is with us and change. It is inevitable that you will not get through this process perfectly the first time. You need these setbacks because they teach you the lessons you need to learn to be successful. This is how you learn. You must view them not as failures but as learning opportunities. You need them to succeed. Remember the old saying, "If at first you don't succeed, try, try again."

It is important that you learn to take risks to be successful in the process of change. If you can remember some of the simple chances you have taken in your personal or organizational life that proved successful, it can help you deal with the risk you find yourself facing now. Think about when you climbed your first tree, rode a two-wheeled bike for the first time, went on your first date, asked your spouse to marry you, had your first child, bought your first car, or applied for your first job. These were all probably scary experiences, but the thrill of success made them all well worth the effort. Risk is an important ingredient of the change process and one you need if you are going to realize meaningful change.

One of the toughest challenges of the change process is the part where you get started. When I begin any process, it often takes me a while to get off the dime. I don't know how many times I sat down to start writing this chapter and then decided to start working on something else simply because I did not know how to get started or where to begin. So, I procrastinated.

Webster's Dictionary says that procrastination is "to put off the doing of something that should be done." Most often fear is at the root of my putting off activities. I may be afraid of failing, or afraid of success. I may be afraid of getting hurt or hurting someone else. Sometimes I don't know what I am afraid of, only that I am afraid. Often times I am afraid that I won't do it perfectly. I get myself in a state where I am so overwhelmed by the fear that I feel powerless to do anything, and that's exactly what I do—nothing. I either sit and wait for it to go away, or I do something completely different, so I won't feel bad about doing nothing. Often doing something else eases the fear and I feel better. When I remember that action helps to erase fear that logic seems to allow me to do what needs to be done rather than an avoidance activity. It is amazing that once I get active the fear subsides, and before I know it, I am into what I should be doing in the first place; the fear magically dissipates.

In many instances the thing I fear the most is that I will not be able to do something perfectly. I am afraid that I will be viewed as flawed, and people will be upset with me and ultimately not like me. Intellectually I know that this is not true; however, emotionally it is a fear that can stop me cold. When it came time to write my doctoral dissertation, at first, I put it off because I didn't know exactly what I wanted to say, and I wanted to get it perfect. Finally, I decided to just sit down and begin to write to see what I would be able to get down on paper. I empowered myself by giving myself the message that even if what I wrote was utter gibberish, I could always go back and rewrite or edit my work. I was surprised how the words began to flow. I found myself saying exactly what I wanted to say, and when I went back and reread my work, I was pleased with how good it was. I have since found that sometimes just the process or activity of doing—doing anything—will provide me with the clarity or idea that is missing when I procrastinate. Just getting active seems to make the project proceed the way it should. I have to remember that I am responsible for the effort and not the outcome. The outcome in most cases is beyond my control. My focus needs to be on doing the best I can and trusting that everything will work out the way it is supposed to. It always seems to work out, and it is usually positive and good for me in the long run.

I taught a graduate course for doctoral students at my university called "Dissertation Boot Camp." I found that there were other doctoral students who had difficulty completing their dissertations, so this class set up a structured support group and resource to help them overcome the challenges of completing this complex work in isolation. In looking for a rallying cry for the members of our boot camp, we borrowed Nike's successful advertising slogan "Just Do It" (1993) and paraphrased our own "Just Write It" The concept worked, and we had an 85 percent dissertation completion rate for the students who participated in the boot camp, far above the national average.

It is easy to get intimidated by the magnitude of the change process that lies before us. Before virtually every marathon I have ever run, I have found myself standing at the starting line asking myself what I am doing. The thought of running nonstop for twenty-six miles can seem awfully foolish. Once that starting gun goes off and the race begins, however, the adrenalin starts to flow, and with each step I am one step closer to being finished.

When I was debating whether or not to apply for an advanced degree, someone said to me, "If you are thinking about an advanced degree, just do it. By the time you finish thinking about it you could be done!" I found that to be true. I was scheduled to begin my doctoral program with a co-worker, who at the last minute thought that maybe this was not the right time because he was too busy at work. I have long since finished my degree, and he is still thinking about it. You will never reach your destination if you don't get started. The sooner you begin, the sooner you will finish.

When getting started in the process of change, it helps to go back and review your goals and desired outcomes. It is beneficial to review the steps or strategies you determined will help you reach your goals and the timetable you have established for completing them. This will help keep you focused on the task at hand. It also helps to remember what the payoff is for successfully achieving this change, so that you will have the motivation to initiate the process. Finally, it is good to remember who is going to help you in this process, so that you remember that you are not really going through this alone; there are others who will help you along the way.

The plan will be more effective if you put pen to paper and document in as much detail as possible what you hope to achieve and how you will achieve it. Some of the questions your plan should answer include:

- Why do you want to make this change? What do you hope to realize as a result of the changes you want to undertake? How will this make your life or organization different and/ or better? What are the specific goals or objectives you want to achieve?

  _____

  _____

  _____

- Where do you want this change to take place? Is there a specific area in your life or in your organization? Is there a specific place or geographic location involved?

  _____

  _____

  _____

- When do you want this change to occur? Is there a specific timeline or deadline that you have in mind or need to ad- here to? When do you anticipate achieving these objectives and goals? What is your specific timeline?

  _____

  _____

  _____

- How will you make all of this happen? What actions must take place for this vision to be realized? What steps can you take to make these changes happen? What actions are out of your hands? What are the specific strategies or steps you will employ?

  _____

  _____

  _____

  _____

- Who is involved in this change besides you? Who else besides you will be affected by the consequences of your change? How will they be affected and how will they react to, or participate in, the process of change? What is their attitude toward these changes? Specifically, who else is involved in the plan, and what is their role?

  _____

  _____

  _____

  _____

- Will there be financial or physical resources required to make this change? What are the specific budget or resource requirements?

  _____

  _____

  _____

- How will you evaluate the success or failure of this plan? What specific metrics will you use to determine success?

  _____

  _____

  _____

You have spent a lot of time thus far getting ready to begin the process of making change. Now it is time to get going. It helps to keep in a positive frame of mind. You may be frightened or intimidated by the journey you are about to embark on; however, remember it is one that you want to make, and it will improve your personal or organizational life. Change is good, and change is necessary. In fact, the only constant in life is that it will change. You can stay where you are for as long as you want, but by your own admission, it is not a place that you want to be.

Remember that in this process, you have already looked at where you are now and determined that you wanted to be someplace else. You have made a commitment to yourself or organization. You have grieved the loss of your present situation and eliminated the unhealthy shame that kept you locked in those uncomfortable old habits for so long. You have mended any fences you have broken or damaged along the way. You have identified and visualized your dream for change and developed a mission or purpose for the journey you will undertake. You have set goals and evaluated your strengths and weaknesses, and you know how you can capitalize on those strengths or compensate for your weaknesses. You have identified where you will need help and have developed and reached out to your network for support. You have outlined the steps necessary and have empowered yourself, or others involved, with the authority to proceed on this journey. It is now time to get going, to be off, and to begin your adventure. Enjoy it, because you have worked hard up to this point, and now is when all the fun begins to happen. If you encounter any difficulties, all you need do is go back, review the process, and rethink the steps.

Get started!

CHAPTER EIGHT

REVIEW & RENEWAL

"Review your goals twice every day in order to focus on achieving them."

LES BROWN

"Life depends on change and renewal."

PATRICK TROUGHTON

It will be important as you proceed along your journey to change that you measure your progress from time to time. There will be times when you get so focused upon your goals that you fail to see just how far you have really come. The process of change is not quick or easy. You may get discouraged along the way and think to yourself, "I just don't feel like I am getting anywhere. Things just don't seem to be any different. This just isn't working!" When it comes to thoughts like this, you will be tempted to give up, but this is when you need to stop and take an objective look at what you have accomplished and just how far you have already progressed.

If you want to have some way of knowing how far you have traveled along the path of making change, it will be helpful to have some sort of monitoring process. It can be complex, or it can be very simple. I think it helps to periodically review your goals and strategies and to analyze just how well they are working. It also helps to have some sort of measurement for us to gauge our progress. In a business the most natural measurements are sales and profits; however, businesses may also keep track of new customers, or new leads or inquiries. A company may also track the quality of its product or service as determined by number of product defects or customer complaints and satisfaction. Progress cannot always be measured in numerical terms.

Researchers, for example, when they conduct experiments record their observations when hard numerical data is not available. You can adopt this system by reflecting on what's happening to you, your situation, or your environment. A daily journal about what you observe as different or what others have observed about your situation can be invaluable in showing you your progress.

Another easy way to monitor your progress is to keep a simple checklist of the steps or strategies that you have determined are critical to successful change. Hopefully, you have developed a timetable for when you expect each step to occur, and a simple checkmark will provide you with a measure to show you how far you have progressed against your plan. Many businesses use checklists as a daily reminder of their progress. It is a good method to remind you of what steps you need to accomplish that day, what you already accomplished, and what remains to be done. One habit I have tried to maintain is at the end of every day to review and update a to-do list I keep on a memo pad. This allows me to see what tasks I have finished that day and gives me a chance to plan for tomorrow's activities.

By monitoring your progress, you will not only have a tool to keep you headed in the right direction when things get tough, but you will also be able to determine if your strategies are working or not. If they are not working up to your satisfaction, you can modify or revise your plan accordingly. If they are exceeding your expectations, you may also want to speed up the process or apply them to another area of your personal or organizational life.

If you are prone to repeating mistakes, monitoring your errors will help you to avoid them as you proceed through the process. The old saying, "those who forget their past are doomed to repeat it" is unfortunately true. Monitoring your actions, evaluating the effect, and taking necessary action are all part of the process that will help to ensure success. Taking things for granted and not paying attention to what is happening around you will guarantee surprises that can greatly upset your forward progress.

Have you ever seen a child with a new toy? At first, they are excited and must play with it every minute of the day. After a few days, they begin to tire of playing with that toy, which is by now an *old thing*, and they start looking for new more exciting things to do. Adults are not too much different. They get a new toy or begin working on a new idea or new process; at first it is exciting and fun, and it seems like they cannot get enough of it. After a while, they begin to tire or lose interest and look for something new to capture their attention.

If you want to make the change process a lasting one, it is important to find ways to keep the spirit of the quest for change alive within you. I have talked much about how I love to run and how important it is in my life. I'm sure by now you are tired of my running analogies, but they work well, so I hope you will bear with me a little longer. To complete a marathon, it is important that you run lots of training miles. The race itself is fun to run. It is an exciting day, usually with lots of people along the route to cheer on the runners. You get caught up in the excitement and the spirit of camaraderie with the other runners, who are sharing your quest for a fun, successful race. But a lot of the training is done alone. You often run the same routes, no one knows who you are, and there are no cheering crowds. Training runs can get old very fast. It is a challenge to get motivated every day; that's why many marathoners know it helps to try different techniques to keep their training runs interesting and exciting. In my case, I joined a running club comprised of people who ran much like I did. I had a number of training partners who kept me company on long runs. We changed the route and location of our long runs to keep them fresh and novel. We even had one long run catered with various delicacies at our water stops along the way.

There are many techniques you can use to keep yourself motivated during the process of change, especially during those times that seem slow, repetitive, or even tedious. We have talked about many of these techniques already. Reviewing your mission often is a good way to stay in tune with your quest for change. Knowing your purpose for making this journey and being committed to it can keep you focused on reaching your objective. We have talked about regularly reviewing your goals to use them as a motivator. Remembering where you have come from and where you want to go can help make getting there that much easier. Not wanting to go back where you have come from will help keep you motivated and focused on your goals, even when facing difficult odds.

The process of change is a lot easier when you are not doing it by yourself. Having other people involved can keep you on track and provide the motivation to keep moving forward when you may not have the energy or enthusiasm yourself.

Making a commitment to yourself and others is another motivating force. When I commit to something out loud to another, I feel obligated to complete the task.

Empowering affirmations can often motivate you when you find yourself running out of steam. A positive thought is often translated into positive action.

It is important to remember when doing anything that the more fun you build into the process the more enjoyable it will be. Given the choice between doing something that is fun and something that is not, you will usually choose the former. We all like to enjoy ourselves, and there is no reason why this process cannot be fun. Remember that the attitude you bring to anything you do will usually determine the level of your enjoyment. The process of change will be fun if you want it to be.

Over the long term, it will be your passion for the process and your quest that will be the primary driving force to keep you moving forward. Passion is that overwhelming feeling of conviction that wells up in us and drives us to succeed. In the process of change, it is critical to fuel that passion and keep it focused on the effort you need to make to achieve your ultimate goals.

There are many things you can do to keep yourself on track, but it is best to remember that you are making change because you ultimately want to be happy and successful. You have embarked on this process to change because you want to advance in your personal or organizational life. If you remember that life is a quest to find your own truth—an adventure into happiness and growth, a process to get you from one stage of life to another—then you can begin to look at change as a positive, healthy, and natural thing. The more positive, exciting, and fun the process the more dedicated you will be to its fulfillment.

The following questions will help you to identify some steps you can take to keep the quest fresh and alive:

- **How passionate are you about making this change?**

  _____

  _____

- **What is your motivation for making the change you are embarking on?**

  _____

  _____

- **What is your level of commitment to making this change?**

  _____

  _____

- **How can you make the change more meaningful?**

  _____

  _____

- **Would making a commitment to another help strengthen your commitment and your resolve to follow through on this process? If so, who would you commit to?**

  _____

  _____

  _____

- How important is your mission in making change, and how can it keep you motivated in reaching your goals?

  _____

  _____

- How can you use a regular review of your goals to keep you focused on attaining them? How often should you re-view your goals?

  _____

  _____

  _____

- What empowering messages can you give yourself to keep you focused on change when the going gets rough?

  _____

  _____

  _____

- What other techniques can you use to help you keep your quest for change alive?

  _____

  _____

- How can you make this process fun?

  _____

  _____

If you have read to this point, hopefully you have come to realize that change is nothing more than a system, requiring your input worked through a process producing an output. At this point, once you have worked through the process outlined on the preceding pages, you should be experiencing the output of that process—results. By simple definition, output is the end result of any process, in this case: change.

Your challenge now is to evaluate that output. Is it what you expected or desired? Does it meet your needs? Are you satisfied with the results? Are there new goals you would like to achieve? How easy or difficult was the process? Is there anything you could have done differently or better? How do you feel about the place you are in right now?

Have you ever wanted something just for the sake of wanting it? I can remember when I was in elementary school, to be really cool you had to dress a certain way. Isn't it funny how some things never change? In any event, in my day the established cool dress was iridescent pants, white-on-white shirts, and black, pointed-toe shoes with metal cleats that protected your heels and made a loud clicking noise when you walked down the street. To top off the outfit you needed to slick back your hair. I was going to private school, and my parents thought it would be more appropriate for me to wear navy blue slacks with a white button-down shirt, official school tie, and plain black loafers with no cleats. They also insisted on short hair, conservatively parted on the left side, unless it was summer when a buzz cut was in order. I wanted to dress like the cool kids in the worst way. All through elementary school I persisted, and my parents resisted. Since they paid for my clothing, I didn't have much of a chance in getting my own way. Finally, when I reached high school, I was working and could afford my own clothes, but the prep look I had sported all those years in elementary school was now cool, and those pointed-toe shoes had given way to penny loafers. Being a closet rebel, however, I walked into a shoe store determined to finally get my pair of pointed-toe shoes with cleats. I found the style I wanted, and much to my amazement, discovered that they looked terrible and felt worse. They pinched my toes, were too narrow, and hurt my feet when I walked. I found out that I didn't really want the shoes as much as I wanted to be able to choose the type of clothing that I was going to wear. I had changed my system from one where clothing purchases were dictated, to one where I could make my own choice; however, I discovered that what I thought was my choice was indeed not what I wanted at all. At the end of the change process, it is not uncommon to find that the output realized may have been what you originally wanted, but as a result of the process, your goals have now changed. If this is the case, you may want to go back to square one, and restart the process with your new goals.

We all want things to go exactly the way we want at any given time. Who in their right mind wants things to go contrary to what they have planned? Unfortunately, Murphy's Law quite often prevails, and anything that can go wrong does! Things are not really as fatalistic as Murphy's Law purports, but you must accept that life is not perfect, and it is unrealistic to expect that things will go exactly as you have planned all the time. It is your responsibility to monitor and evaluate what is happening in your personal or organizational life so you can prevent minor deviations from turning into disasters. It is for this reason that you need to measure your progress. If you are diligent and stay on top of things, you can better ensure that your progress is going in the direction you want it to.

An important part of evaluating the output of the change process is determining the value of that output. It is important to assess the value received from the output in material, financial, mental, emotional, and spiritual terms. For example, if one output of the process is a deeper understanding of yourself, your value system, and your potential as a person, what would the emotional, mental, and spiritual value of that understanding be? If your process of change involved moving your organization from an outdated method of operation to a more contemporary model, what would the value of that output be in increased productivity and profit to the company? By assigning value to the output you can better determine the effectiveness and worth of the process.

Another element to evaluate is the consequences of the output realized. Consequences, your end results or effects of the change process, are important to assess because you will want to review these consequences and their implications on input as you recycle the change process. We will discuss this further in the next chapter.

If you determine that the output of this process of change is not what you desire, then it is simply a matter of going back to stage one and retracing your steps to see where things went astray and what you can do differently to affect a different result. If you determine that the output of the process is exactly what you want, then it is time to identify the next issue you want to address and begin the process again. It is important to remember that this is a process not a destination. Change is a constant; therefore, you are never really finished with the process, merely recycling it to work on the next issue or challenge you face.

Webster's defines feedback as "the transfer of part of the output back to input ... as in information." Once again, your friends at Merriam-Webster are right on point in linking their definition to the process of change. If any process is to be successful, especially one that is constantly recycling itself, it is essential that information about the success or failure of the process be transferred back as input for further consideration and refinement. In the context of the process presented here, feedback is vital information about the consequences or results of the process that is fed back to the input phase of the system to help make better decisions about how change can be realized more effectively and successfully.

You give and get feedback daily. For example, if you are in a grumpy mood in the morning, your family, friends, associates, and even your pets are usually quick to give you feedback on how your grumpiness is affecting their day. It may not be in a form that is politically correct, but lines like "look who woke up on the wrong side of the bed this morning" generally give us a quick read on the consequences our current behavior has generated. Parents are always giving their children positive and negative feedback on how their current behavior fits in with their view of appropriate conduct. Supervisors give their employees feedback on how they are performing on the job in the form of reviews, praise for work well done, and reprimands for poor work or inappropriate behavior. Feedback is necessary for you to know if the actions you employed were successful or not in producing the result you desired.

Feedback is necessary for all of us. We all have blind spots that can cause us to behave in certain ways, both positive and negative. All too often you do not even know you are behaving in this manner or the consequences of your actions. I remember when my company sent me to a weeklong workshop to learn how to make more effective presentations. Most of the workshop was spent making actual presentations, which were videotaped and then critiqued by the class and the workshop leader. On the first day, without any prior notice, we were told we had to make a five-minute ad lib presentation on any subject that we wanted. I gave my presentation convinced that a river of sweat was pouring down my face and that I was visibly shaking, taking extremely long pauses, stammering my words, and boring everyone in the group. I was sure that each and every person in the session could see the blind panic in my eyes. After I finished speaking, the workshop leader played back the tape. I was amazed to see a person who looked extremely relaxed, who very articulately delivered his presentation in an easy-going manner, and who had the interest of the class with an entertaining and funny presentation. This feedback was unlike any I had ever received before. The tape showed me blind spots that I could not possibly see by myself. This feedback changed the way I viewed making presentations. I realized that if I was well prepared and had a subject that the audience was interested in, then they would be on my side, wanting me to be interesting. I also realized that I was very competent in my presentation style. What was once a traumatic task became a labor of love and opened the way for me to get into teaching.

Feedback can be internal as well as external. By conducting an internal evaluation of your behavior and the resulting consequences, you can make some determinations about what went right and what went wrong, what you like and what you did not like, and what you consider success and what you consider failure. The key to internal feedback is honesty. If we are in denial about those actions or behaviors that do not work for us, we are not likely to correct them. We need to be honest about those that do work for us as well. False humility can be just as damaging as denial. We need feedback for what it can show us about ourselves. We need the information from both inside and outside of ourselves in an objective unbiased manner.

Think about how important feedback has been to you or your organization. Feedback may have helped you form impressions of other people or organizations. It may have helped you to clarify important issues that affected your personal or organizational life. It may have even helped motivate you to undertake the change process in which you now find yourself. Feedback is essential if you are going to be more informed, more effective, and more successful. You need to seek it out and welcome it from any source, both internal and external.

CHAPTER NINE

APPLYING THE PROCESS TO ALL AREAS OF YOUR LIFE

"To improve is to change; to be perfect is to change often."

WINSTON CHURCHILL

A t this point in the process, you should have experienced some meaningful change either personally or organizationally. You have looked at one or more areas of your life, and by making the necessary input and working the process, you have realized output that was to your liking. The general tendency right now is to sit back, admire your work, and relax for a while. Unfortunately, life keeps chugging along and won't allow you to sit around for too long before it throws another challenge your way. You need to welcome these challenges, as they are opportunities for growth and change.

Your old friend Merriam-Webster defines recycle as "to pass again through a series of changes or treatments." This system of change will only be as successful as the amount of effort you put into it and the manner in which you use it. It is built to be used over and over to address the myriad of challenges that will present themselves over the course of your personal and organizational life.

There is an old saying: "What goes around comes around." The process of change is a recycling system that keeps on going around and around. It is not something that you do once and are done with. It is a system for dealing with the ongoing cycle of change that is part of the existence that we call life. All people and all organizations are constantly in the process of change. The problem is that you don't always recognize that fact. Your body ages every day. Your children get bigger every day. You form new relationships with people on a daily basis. Your organization expands and shrinks and makes or loses money daily. The only constant is that things will continue to change.

I have been using this process in my own life and those of my clients since 1976. Over that period of time, I have never personally, or met anyone else for that matter, who has finished the process of personal or organizational development and growth. On second thought I do know of a few people; however, they are all dead.

My own personal philosophy is that we all exist here in this life to learn how to become better people. I think that philosophy translates well into organizations as well. They exist to learn how to better serve their customers, employees, and society at large while being self-sustaining and producing an adequate return on investment. If you look at the most successful and healthy organizations and individuals, they never seem to be satisfied with the status quo. They are always looking for ways to improve, to learn, and to grow. They know that they will be happier and more fulfilled if they continue to grow and develop than if they get complacent and remain where they are. They are always changing, always in transition. The difference I have seen between successful people and organizations, and those that are not, is that the successful ones have a system that works for them, and they apply it to everything they do. Once you have experienced a change process that works, you can apply it to every area of your personal and organizational life.

If you have been putting this process to work, by now you should be seeing some results in your efforts to change. Hopefully it has instilled in you a renewed confidence in yourself and your abilities. Hopefully it has shown you that this process does indeed work and that you can affect change in any area of your personal or professional life. If you are at that point, you are at the final step in the process.

Have you ever gotten good news when there was no one around to share it with? You get this feeling inside that if you don't tell someone your news quickly you will bust. And if you cannot find someone to talk to about your great news, doesn't some of the excitement and fun seem to go out of the whole process?

Much of the joy in making change lies in the ability to share the benefit of that change with others. I have often gone through periods and situations requiring change in my life, and at the time I could not figure out why. It was not until sometime later when talking to a family member, friend, or acquaintance who found themselves in a similar situation that I realized my experience could help that person get through the change much easier and more effectively. I realized that, if for no other reason, I could justify my experience and the effort I made in the fact that I could use my knowledge to help someone else. I can usually find other reasons why I need to make change, but I find a lot of comfort, satisfaction, and esteem in being able to help another through my experience. There is no better gift you can give another than the means to make their life better.

Earlier in the book I wrote about Abraham Maslow and his hierarchy of needs. The pinnacle of his needs pyramid was self-actualization, where your true creative nature is realized and the true meaning of your life holds deep and meaningful purpose for you. Scott Barry Kaufman (2020), in his book *Transcend: The New Science of Self-Actualization*, studied Maslow and other prominent scholars. He wrote that Maslow, in his later years, believed that "healthy self-realization was a bridge to transcendence. He describes transcendence as moments "in which awareness was expanded beyond the self . . . motivated by higher values." Maslow believed that those who self-actualize "tend to be altruistic, creative, open, authentic, accepting, independent, and brave." In transcendence they use these attributes not to benefit self, but to benefit others. In the case of change, self-actualized people transcend through this process and share the benefits of the knowledge and experience gained through the change process with others.

There is a deeper reason why it is important to share your experience with others. In the retelling you revisit, re-experience, and reinforce the stages of the process that got you where you are. You remind yourself why it was that you made the change in the first place, what steps you took to get you to your desired goals, and what was the ultimate outcome. In essence, you reaffirm the process and motivate yourself to make further change. When I talk to someone else, I am the first person who hears what I have to say. I often find that in sharing my story with others I am telling others what I most need to hear. By talking about the process that resulted in positive change, you are in effect keeping the change process alive in yourself. You are constantly reminding yourself that change is good, and it brings with it positive rewards.

CHAPTER TEN

CONCLUSION

"A conclusion is the place where you get tired of thinking."

ARTHUR BLOCH

Hopefully one of the things you have learned from this book is that change does not have to be an overwhelming, mind-boggling, threatening, or traumatic experience for you. If you approach it as a systematic event, identify the necessary input, and diligently work the stages of the process, then you will realize a positive output. If you have learned how the process of change can positively impact your life. or that of your organization, then my work here has been worthwhile. I am grateful that you have taken the time to review and experience this document, and my hope for you is that you continue to realize and enjoy all the positive changes that are coming in your life. I have lived a life worth remembering; hopefully you will too! Good luck and good fortune.

"The secret of change is to focus all your energy not on fighting the old, but on building the new…"

SOCRATES

RESOURCES

Bradshaw, John. *Healing the Shame That Binds You*. New York: Bantam Books, 1989.

Capra, Frank. *It's a Wonderful Life*. Los Angeles, CA: Republic Pictures, 1946.

Collins, Jim. *Good to Great*. New York: Harper Collins Publishers, 2001.

Devanna, Mary Anne, Charles J. Fombrun, and Noel M. Tichy. "Strategic Human Resource Management." Cambridge, MA: Sloan Management Review, 1982.

Drucker, Peter F. An *Introductory View of Management*. New York: Harper College Press, 1977.

Grenny, Joseph, David Maxwell, Ron McMillan, Kerry Patterson, and Al Switzler. *Influencer: The Power to Change Anything*. New York: McGraw-Hill, 2008.

Jacobs, Ronald L. "Systems Theory Applied to Human Resource Development." Alexandria, VA: American Society for Training and Development, 1989.

Kaufman, Scott Barry. *Transcend: The New Science of Self-Actualization*. New York: Tarcher Perigee, 2020.

Keane, Bil. *The Family Circus*. New York: Coles Syndication, 1993.

Keirsey, David and Marilyn Bates. *Please Understand Me, Character and Temperament Types*. Carlsbad, CA: Prometheus Nemesis Book Company, 1984.

Kübler-Ross, Elizabeth. *On Death and Dying*, New York: Simon & Schuster/Touchstone, 1969.

Marcum, David and Steven Smith. *Egonomics: What Makes Ego Our Greatest Asset (or Most Expensive Liability)*. New York: Fireside, 2007.

Maslow, Abraham. *Motivation and Personality*. New York: Harper & Row, 1954.

Meyers Briggs, Isabel. *Gifts Differing*. Palo Alto, CA: Consulting Psychologists' Press, 1980.

Mish, Frederick C., ed. *Webster's Collegiate Dictionary*, Tenth Edition. Springfield, MA: Merriam-Webster, 1996.

Peale, Dr. Norman Vincent. *The Power of Positive Thinking*. New York: Prentice Hall, 1952.

Senge, Peter M. *The Fifth Discipline: The Art & Practice of the Learning Organization*. New York: Doubleday/Currency, 1990.

Tolkien, J.R.R. *The Hobbit*. Santa Monica, CA: Xenon Video, 1991.

Weiden, Dan. "Just Do It." Eugene, OR: Wieden & Kennedy for Nike, 1993.

ABOUT THE AUTHOR

JOHN J. KING, Ed.D.

D r. John J. King can be best described as an author, educator, entrepreneur, futurist, innovator, marketer, strategist, and leader. He earned a Bachelor of Arts in economics from St. Bernard College, a Master of Education and Certificate in Organizational Development from the University of Minnesota, and a Doctorate in Educational Leadership from the University of St. Thomas. He is a highly accomplished and proven senior executive, C-suite officer, entrepreneur, consultant, provost, dean, professor, and board member with significant success in higher education, academia, and adult education as well as in the airline, manufacturing, international trade, advertising, and retail sectors.

Leveraging his extensive experience in leadership and executive management, Dr. King is a valuable asset for a range of companies looking for acumen in leadership and organizational development as well as strategic planning. His broad areas of expertise include entrepreneurship; executive consulting, coaching and mentoring; profit and loss management; financial analysis and budgets; brand marketing; organizational effectiveness; distance and blended learning; e-learning; corporate training; program and curriculum development; academic administration; accreditation; operations management; regulatory and legal compliance; process and quality improvement; and high-performance team building.